The Seven Redemptive Names of Christ Jesus

Apostle Cheryl Fortson

Life On Purpose Publishing
SAN ANTONIO, TEXAS

The Seven Redemptive Names of Christ Jesus

Apostle Cheryl Fortson

Apostle Cheryl Fortson
apostlecheryl@comcast.net

Scripture quotations marked AMP are from the Holy Bible: *The Amplified Bible.* 1987. 2015. La Habra, CA: The Lockman Foundation.

Ordering Information:
Quantity sales. Special discounts are available on quantity purchases by ministries, associations, and others. For details, contact the author at the email address above.

A Gap Closer ™ Publication
A Division of Life On Purpose Publishing
San Antonio, Texas

The Seven Redemptive Names of Christ Jesus/
Apostle Cheryl Fortson
ISBN 13: 978-1-7336950-4-6

DEDICATION

I would like to dedicate this book first to the Lord of my life, Christ Jesus the author and finisher of my faith. From a very young girl I have been aware of His faithfulness and protection towards me during every stage of my life.

I would also like to dedicate this book to my husband, Pastor John Sr. who stands with me in ministry. I thank God for you and to my very committed adult children who also serve with us in ministry, Pastor John Jr., our Children's Pastor; Pastor Darryl Sr., our Youth Pastor and his wife, Prophet Christine; and our daughter Deacon Chervon who has always encouraged me and serves wherever she can; she also serves in our church's hair salon. "You are always seeing after me and your Father at church and at home." My family is the best!

I would also like to dedicate this book to our awesome twelve grandchildren and our great grandchildren, our godchildren and spiritual sons and daughters in the faith who pray for me and many of you also serve with me in our ministry.

I also dedicate this book to the greatest Apostle, Dad and friend in this world, my overseer, the Anointed Apostle, Dr. John E. Wilson who is always there for me. I love and appreciate you. Dad.

To my family, the Fortsons and the Fothergills and church family, Full Gospel Foundation Building Ministry International, I love and thank each one of you for praying for me, loving and serving in ministry with me. You all confirm the apostolic call on my life.

Lastly, I would also like to dedicate this book to the late Helen and Gerald Fothergill, Sr. They were the parents that God chose to bring me into this world for purpose and destiny. My mom, whom people called Sissy, taught me how to love everybody I meet. I watched her endless expressions and acts of love towards others. My Dad, whom people called Jerry, taught me integrity and consistency in my work ethic. They both were very gifted people and passed greatness onto all eleven of their children.

Thank you, Lord Jesus, for blessing my life with so many people that helped to influence me for purpose, and all that You assign me to do in this life.

ACKNOWLEDGMENTS

Words cannot express the appreciation and love I have in my heart for one of the most anointed churches in the world, Full Gospel Foundation Building Ministries International of Bloomfield, Connecticut. You have confirmed that I am one of God's end time apostles.

You have supported me and my family at Full Gospel through everything that we have grown through! I never leave your presence without telling you that I love you, you make it so easy to love you.

I give a special thanks to all my family members who serve faithfully with your gifts, talents and finances in Full Gospel. Pastors Deborah and Bryan, my sister-in-love and my brother, you are the best; my brother, Deacon Clayvern, you use your excellent gifts wherever you are needed. You all make my life easy.

I want to thank the following people for inspiring me to sit down and find time to write my second book, Minister Yvette Owens for finding all the right people to help me get this book published. Minister Sheila Harris, thank you for transcribing this book and all the hard work and hours you spent making all the changes and corrections. Also, I would like to thank my two cousins Minister Donna and Prophet Andrea who designed this beautiful book cover. Thanks to my anointed armorbearers who faithfully take care of me with unconditional love; Prophet Gwen, Minister Joyce, Minister LaVerne and Minister Yvonne who fills in without the title. I could not do what I do without each one of you serving with me in Full Gospel.

Love you,
Apostle Cheryl

CONTENTS

FOREWORD

A POSTLE, "APÓSTOLOS" IN the Greek, sounds so phenomenal and formidable! After all, isn't that what they called those early "church guys" that followed Jesus around performing miracles and living those incredible-to-believe lives? If you put that in today's vernacular, you're getting something that seems even more portentous! As remarkable a word as apostle may seem to some, it is even more remarkable to interact with a real one face to face in modern times!

This book you are about to sentiently experience is written by a latter-day apostle from the perspective of the apostolic. What a delicious way to learn about the power in the covenant names of our Lord and Saviour and His

Father! "How sweet are thy words unto my taste! Yea, sweeter than honey to my mouth!" Psalm 119:103 (KJV). Quite a bit to think about; a lot to take in, isn't it? I mean to muse over the fact that our Father dictates something through our mortality that changes our lives in profound ways, drawing us closer to His immortality!

"But you, O man of God, flee these things and pursue righteousness, godliness, faith, love, patience, gentleness. Fight the good fight of faith, lay hold on eternal life, to which you were also called and have confessed the good confession in the presence of many witnesses. I urge you in the sight of God who gives life to all things, and *before* Christ Jesus who witnessed the good confession before Pontius Pilate, that you keep *this* commandment without spot, blameless until our Lord Jesus Christ's appearing, which He will manifest in His own time, *He who is* the blessed and only Potentate, the King of kings and Lord of lords, who alone has immortality, dwelling in unapproachable light, whom no man has seen or can see, to whom *be* honor and everlasting power. Amen." I Timothy 6:11-16 (NKJV)

Now that's an extraordinary thought! Wow! I hope I've spoiled it for you just reading this like just anyone wrote it and it's just another humdrum Christian book. You can only read something like this with an eye hungry for revelation and a heart ready to apply it to the working mechanisms of your life that aspire you to greatness. This was written through the blood sweat and tears of a true apostle. Yes, this written manuscript is a love letter from heaven through the eyes of that apostle, the kind of love letter that instructs and innervates you to enter into another dimension of understanding. You need to enter another dimension of understanding!

One of the Lord's covenant names (covered more thoroughly than my meager attempts) according to this book is "Jehovah Shammah." This name is referenced in Ezekiel as one of the last cities designated for the lands governed by the 12 tribes of Israel. "The circumference of the city shall be eighteen thousand cubits. And the name of the city from that time on shall be, "The Lord is There." (Ezekiel 48:35 NKJV)

That is its meaning, "the Lord is there," connoting His omnipresence in all things. Apostle Fortson could have written 1,000 pages on this one name alone and not exhausted the subject. How powerful is that? Israel needed to create a memorial to God after their harrowing journey to freedom that would signify that He is the end-all, the absolute reason why they were able to come into the land promised them in the time of Moses. Whenever they spoke this name, they evoked the presence of God into position to win battles, lift their spirits, inhabit their homes and bless their efforts in all things. How annihilative invoking this name was to the enemies of Israel and presently to your enemies as well. Picture this: Each time they (and we) confessed this name He caused great memories of victory, peace and power to fill their minds. It reminded them from whence they came and assured them of a future of brilliance bringing to mind that with God nothing is impossible. With their God, and no one else's. There is no God like Jehovah, then or now.

This is but one of the seven redemptive names of the Lord who caresses and shelters our lives in His arresting love and presence. We're going to learn a lot more as we study the others as though we are seeing them for the first time. There's a problem that I've observed over the years in the Body of Christ: Somehow, we think that since we read another similar book, we don't need to read this one. That's as useless a thought as, because some of us may be apostles we don't need an apostle in our lives! It is a good thing that your doctor didn't feel that way when his physician ministered life to him so that he could yours! There I go again, getting you to consider things you didn't deem necessary to "give it a thought." Well since we're on the subject, shouldn't you be thinking about the wonderful and compelling truths you're about to learn through the pages of this book?

By now you should be salivating to read what God may have spoken to you personally through this writer.

So, what are you waiting for? "Jehovah Jireh" the provider to all of the universe, has given you this gift from His throne to enjoy. Feast with gladness and gratitude that my friend, Cheryl Fortson, stopped her life long enough to freely give you a precious moment of it to enrich yours. Now, it's time to begin the study of "the Seven Redemptive Names of Christ Jesus." I'm excited to start, aren't you?

Pam Vinnett

INTRODUCTION

HOLY SPIRIT, THE Master Teacher and revelator of God's Word has given me some awesome revelations concerning how to properly appropriate our redemptive Covenant Blessings for divine healing and health. God has a supernatural process in His covenant for receiving divine health. I am so excited that divine healing and divine health is in the Lord's covenant because of God's atonement available for His Church.

Therefore, this covenant benefit is not anything that a believer has to beg God for. It belongs to every new covenant believer and the only reason that we would not walk in God's gift of divine health and wholeness according to the Word is because we are not exercising our faith for it.

Divine health came out of the Finished Works of Calvary's Cross. The all-powerful and precious Blood of the Lamb paid for this benefit in full. God's favor is on our lives. I have learned that the very first thing to do when a person is experiencing sickness in their body is to get revelation from the teaching ministry of Holy Spirit concerning what the Word of God says about divine health and healing for the believers. It is our redemptive covenant right to be made whole! Our redemption is the currency of Heaven, we have every right to access all our covenant provisions.

> *Romans 8:11 (AMP)*
>
> *11 And if the Spirit of Him Who raised up Jesus from the dead dwells in you, [then] He Who raised up Christ Jesus from the dead will also restore to life your mortal (short-lived, perishable) bodies through His Spirit Who dwells in you.*

Holy Spirit is on an earthly assignment to quicken and restore our physical bodies and keep them whole, we have work to do for the Kingdom of God.

The scriptures declare that our bodies are the Temples of God and He has commanded us to bring honor and glory to Him in our bodies.

Therefore, God through His Son Christ Jesus has made provisions through His Seven Redemptive Names for every new covenant believer's health.

It is time that every Believer understands that "the divine healer" lives on the inside of us and it is past time that we walk in our full inheritance in Christ. The Body of Christ is a new species of super humans that has never existed before. The Godhead lives in us to reveal Christ through us to this confused world.

I finally understand that everything we will ever need here on earth is already inside of us through Christ Jesus, our Lord. His name is Jehovah, the I AM that I AM! Christ Jesus is everything that we will ever need throughout eternity.

All the Lord is waiting for from us is to give Him His sword, the spoken Word of God coming out of our mouths in faith. Our positive response is the substance that He needs to release every covenant promise in our lives and His Promises are in these Seven Redemptive Names of Christ Jesus.

The substitutionary sacrifice of Christ Jesus has qualified every new covenant believer to receive all of the benefits connected to "The Seven Redemptive Names of Christ Jesus."

The Seven Redemptive Names of Christ Jesus

Jehovah Shammah – The Lord our ever-present God, who dwells within every born-again believer, we are Temples of God's glory.

Jehovah Shalom – The Lord is our Shalom peace and well-being. There is nothing missing, broken or lacking. We are Complete in Him.

Jehovah Rohi – The Lord is our chief shepherd, the great shepherd of His flock. He died and gave his life for us and we are always protected by Him.

Jehovah Jireh – The Lord is our Provider. He knows and provides everything we need before we ever need it.

Jehovah Nissi – The Lord is our banner and victor over every situation in this life. The Lord is our Triumphant warrior.

Jehovah Tisidkenu – The Lord is our righteousness. Through God's gift of righteousness, every believer possesses the power to be transformed and fully restored to God and every provision in the kingdom is now ours.

Jehovah Rapha – The Lord is our Divine Healer. He restores, delivers and heals us, spirit, soul and body so that we can walk in our divine purpose whole.

PREFACE

ROMANS 8:11

¹¹ And if the Spirit of Him Who raised up Jesus from the dead dwells in you, [then] He Who raised up Christ Jesus from the dead will also restore to life your mortal (short-lived, perishable) bodies through His Spirit Who dwells in you.

The Spirit of the Lord spoke these words to me one day, "I want my **Church** whole, spirit, soul and body." The Lord did not want us to go from healing to healing but spiritually and physically whole. Because of His finished works on Calvary's Cross, every believer has inherited the right to the promises in this scripture. This is our Lord's executive order that must be carried out by us daily.

The same Spirit that raised up the body of Christ Jesus over 2,000 years ago from the dead, is the same Spirit that dwells inside of every New Covenant Believer in Christ today.

Colossians 2:10

10 And you are in Him, made full and having come to fullness of life [in Christ you too are filled with the Godhead—Father, Son and Holy Spirit—and reach full spiritual stature]. And He is the Head of all rule and authority [of every angelic principality and power].

The purpose for this Book is to allow Holy Spirit to bring present-day truths to the Church about how He has been assigned to teach us how to allow Him through the redemption of Christ Jesus to quicken our bodies every day to health and wholeness. To quicken us means to restore us, to recover us, to repair us, to revive us, and to make us well through God's Supernatural zoë life flowing within us.

This is absolutely possible because our new covenant declares that we are the temples of God here on earth.

I Corinthians 6:19-20

[19] Do you not know that your body is the temple (the very sanctuary) of the Holy Spirit Who lives within you, Whom you have received [as a Gift] from God? You are not your own,

[20] You were bought with a price [purchased with a preciousness and paid for, [b]made His own]. So then, honor God and bring glory to Him in your body

This is how you can honor God and bring glory to Him in your body as you allow the revelations in this book given to me by Holy Spirit about the Seven Redemption Names of Christ Jesus to become a reality. I have been taught by Holy Spirit that we can legally walk in divine health and wholeness every day of our lives here on earth.

These past few years have been the most challenging years of my life. My body and mind have been under severe attacks from the enemy. The Lord spoke to me one day when I wanted to literally give up on life and said, "Cheryl, you have too much of my Word in you to give up now!" He reminded me of my supernatural encounter in 1984.

I began to hear the Holy Spirit remind me that I have a full redemption, an everlasting release from the entire curse. No one is authorized to say that the Redemptive Names of Christ Jesus is not for the Body of Christ today.

Who can change God's I AM to I was! Christ is Shammah, the Glory of God in us. Christ is Shalom, our perfect Peace and well-being. Christ is Rohi, our Chief Shepherd who gave His life for us. Christ is Jireh, our eternal provider Christ is Nissi, our triumphant Banner and Victor. Christ is Tisidkenu, our eternal gift of Righteousness and Christ is Rapha, our Healer and divine health, right now! Don't ever forget Christ Jesus is the same yesterday today and forever more.

1 MY STORY

EARLY ONE MORNING in January 1984, like the Apostle Paul, I had what I call an "out of body experience" with God that took me into the presence of Christ Jesus. This encounter would change my life forever. Every part of this supernatural visitation has imprinted itself in my heart, and I can describe every part of it in detail, even today.

How awesome it was to hear the voice of both our Heavenly Father and then our Lord, Jesus Christ. Abba spoke to me while my spirit was still on earth in my bedroom. I was awakened out of my sleep; I knew that it was very early even though I never opened my eyes. At first, I thought my husband, John, was calling my name. After I heard my name, I then heard these words, "Cheryl, I am calling you to teach and preach my word and to heal the sick." I then realized that this was an audible voice, but it was not my husband; he was still at work at the firehouse. It was God giving me directives concerning His purpose and plan for my life. Yes, this encounter would change the direction of my life forever!

I remember asking, "Lord, how can I get people healed when I can't even get my own body healed?" I had been experiencing a lot of demonic attacks against my body and mind. One of the enemy's severe attacks against me was chronic eczema. I was not born with eczema but broke out all over my body after a trauma I experienced in my youth. I would not find out until many years later that my attacks of eczema were a direct result of emotional dysfunction triggered by constant fear. In fact, this fear caused me to experience phobias of every kind, especially fear of the dark, fear of cats, and fear of death.

The enemy tormented me for many years as I battled severe health issues. The shame I experienced throughout my teenage years because of the outbreaks of eczema caused me to hide my body and develop a spirit of rejection which affected me in several ways. The spirit of rejection triggered my out-of-control emotions, which triggered chemical imbalances, which triggered severe outbreaks of eczema. I developed a goiter caused by an enlarged thyroid gland. I developed respiratory lung problems which created asthmatic symptoms. I also had cataracts and floaters in my eyes. These are just a few of the attacks against my health. Now perhaps you can better understand why I questioned the Lord and His call for me to minister healing to the sick. I considered how much warfare I was already experiencing trying to learn how to get my body healed, and that was why my response was, "Lord, how can I pray for the sick when I can't figure out how to get my own body healed?" I even questioned who would believe *me* for their healing.

Immediately after I responded to the Lord, He replied, "I will teach you how to get your body healed." I then saw myself standing directly in front of Jesus in heaven. His entire body was clothed in God's glory. His white robe was a white that I had never seen before; it was glowing. His eyes were so loving and all I could do was weep. Even as I write this chapter and share my experience with you, the memory of His eyes still causes me to weep.

I looked only at Him even though I could see other things going on around me at the same time. I could see sick people in beds with sheets over them. There were people of every race, age and gender with all kinds of sicknesses and diseases. Jesus instructed me to lay hands on each one of them. It seemed like there were thousands of people to be healed. I remember that even though I could see the people being healed, I never took my focus off Jesus who was standing directly in front of me. It was not until He told me to look behind me that I shifted my gaze and saw what looked like a multitude of healed people. I heard these words, "They will follow you as you follow Christ Jesus," and immediately I was back on earth in my body.

That same morning, Holy Spirit prompted me to call my pastor and make an appointment so I could share this life-changing experience with him. My pastor chose the date for my first sermon on Mother's Day, May 13,1984. I released a powerful message on "The Trinity of God." My pastor said to the congregation that in all the years of his life in ministry he had never heard a more powerful and mature word delivered in a person's first sermon. I give God all the glory, praise, and thanksgiving for the teaching ministry of Holy Spirit in my life. He has held first place of authority in my life even until this day!

A few years later I joined another church where I started to do ministry full time. I had such a hunger for God's Word. I studied the scriptures daily and learned how to make faith confessions over myself, my family and others. My pastor assigned me to teach Bible Study, to minister at our Wednesday noon Miracle Services and our Tuesday 6:00 a.m. morning prayer, where God used me to heal the sick and to teach and preach the Gospel. Many people who came to the Wednesday Noon Day services on their lunch hour would get saved, healed and grew spiritually in the Word. In those days of being perfected for full time ministry, I went into nursing homes, hospitals, and people's homes to pray for the sick and to serve them the Holy Communion meal weekly.

My faith in the substitutionary work of Calvary's Cross grew tremendously and I saw so many signs, wonders, and miracles. For example, people with all different types of diseases were healed. I prayed for a woman unable to conceive. Some months later she and her beautiful baby boy came to see me. She wanted me to know that God healed her of lupus and opened her womb. A woman stood proxy for her husband who needed a heart transplant. He was healed and received a new heart. A few years later he came to thank me for praying for him, and to show me that God had healed him. God showed him in a vision who I was and even what I would be wearing because he had never seen me before. He came to show me that God had healed him in that service that day when his wife stood proxy for him.

In 1994, ten years later, God spoke to me concerning pioneering our church, Full Gospel Foundation Building

APOSTLE CHERYL FORTSON

Ministries International of Bloomfield, Connecticut. God said He would use our church to be a resource center to perfect the Body of Christ to do the work of the ministry under the doctrinal teachings of the Apostles and Prophets. Christ Jesus would always be the center cornerstone of our church according to Ephesians 2:20. The Spirit of God is still true to His prophetic word spoken to me in 1984 because He still uses me to teach and preach the Gospel of Grace, heal the sick, and bring deliverance to people.

God began to train Full Gospel through His perfecting process by anointing us to raise up a very successful Christian school called the *Foot Soldiers Academy of Destiny* for children in Kindergarten through the twelfth grade. This was indeed a miracle because people don't normally start a school with all 12 grades at one time. I believe that the only reason that we were successful is because it was the will of God for our church. We were able to give the children spiritual training as well as excellent academic education. A few years later God would anoint us to open our *Perfecting School of Ministry Bible Training Center* that is still blessing leaders and laity today. This Holy Spirit-filled accredited bible school is presently offering the associate and bachelor's degrees as well as our Kingdom Business School and our third-level Ministry perfecting classes which also help the Spirit of God to equip the Five-Fold Ministry Gifts.

THE SEVEN REDEMPTIVE NAMES OF CHRIST JESUS

God has anointed and appointed me to teach and train the Body of Christ during our Wednesday evening mid-week services. I often release God's present-day truths concerning His Covenant of Healing and divine health for the Body of Christ. I believe the Body of Christ should walk in divine health and wholeness so that we can obey God's mandate for His new covenant church concerning His Great Commission revealed in Mark 16:15-20 (AMP).

Mark 16:15-20 (AMP)

15 And He said to them, Go into all the world and preach and publish openly the good news (the Gospel) to every creature [of the whole human race].

16 He who believes [who adheres to and trusts in and relies on the Gospel and Him Whom it sets forth] and is baptized will be saved [from the penalty of eternal death]; but he who does not believe [who does not adhere to and trust in and rely on the Gospel and Him Whom it sets forth] will be condemned.

17 And these attesting signs will accompany those who believe: in My name they will drive out demons; they will speak in new languages;

18 They will pick up serpents; and [even] if they drink anything deadly, it will not hurt them; they will lay their hands on the sick, and they will get well.

19 So then the Lord Jesus, after He had spoken to them, was taken up into heaven and He sat down at the right hand of God.

20 And they went out and preached everywhere, while the Lord kept working with them and confirming the message by the attesting signs and miracles that closely accompanied [it]. Amen (so be it).

We cannot obey this mandate for the Lord's Church if we ourselves are sick. We must believe that the Word of God is spirit and zóé life. It penetrates our spirit when we declare it. When we renew our minds with God's word, it will always heal our bodies. I believe our physical bodies continue to be quickened to health by the power of God's Spirit and Word when we submit to His eternal Word. The ministry that God revealed to me during that divine encounter with Him in January 1984 is the exact ministry of Christ Jesus when He walked the earth. The spirit of God has called me to "teach and preach and heal the sick" according to Matthew 4:23-25 (AMP).

Matthew 4:23-25 (AMP)

23 And He went about all Galilee, teaching in their synagogues and preaching the good news (Gospel) of the kingdom, and healing every disease and every weakness and infirmity among the people.

24 So the report of Him spread throughout all Syria, and they brought Him all who were sick, those afflicted with various diseases and torments, those under the power of demons, and epileptics, and paralyzed people, and He healed them.

25 And great crowds joined and accompanied Him about, coming from Galilee and Decapolis [the district of the ten cities east of the Sea of Galilee] and Jerusalem and Judea and from the other [the east] side of the Jordan.

It is also very clear to me now why the enemy waged such a fierce attack on my physical health. I believe everything that has taken place in my life has prepared me to fulfill God's mandate for my ministry on earth. I am positively convinced that Christ Jesus through His Spirit inside of me is the source of divine healing and health that is quickening my body to wholeness every new day so that I can obey God's perfect will for my life. Let's look at this proof in Romans 8:11.

Romans 8:11

11 And if the Spirit of Him Who raised up Jesus from the dead dwells in you, [then] He Who raised up Christ Jesus from the dead will also restore to life your mortal (short-lived, perishable) bodies through His Spirit Who dwells in you.

Saints, I am equipped to live out the days of my life on earth "teaching, preaching and healing the sick because the Godhead lives inside of me." Now go with me to another scripture that will prove this in Colossians 2:10 (AMP).

Colossians 2:10

10 And you are in Him, made full and having come to fullness of life [in Christ you too are filled with the Godhead—Father, Son and Holy Spirit—and reach full spiritual stature]. And He is the Head of all rule and authority [of every angelic principality and power].

As you read this book, I ask you to meditate on every scripture because the Word of God is going to build your faith to receive every covenant promise included in the seven redemptive names of Christ Jesus. This is the process Holy Spirit taught me and instructed me to use to get my body healed. My healing came through the powerful anointings of Jehovah Shammah's presence and His glory inside of me; Jehovah Shalom's Peace and well-being in me; Jehovah Rohi as my Chief Shephard and Protector;

THE SEVEN REDEMPTIVE NAMES OF CHRIST JESUS

Jehovah Jireh, my Provider and Source, who meets my every need; Jehovah Nissi my Banner and Victor who fights every battle for me as my triumphant warrior; Jehovah Tisidkenu my Gift of Righteousness which is my new identity in Christ and Jehovah Rapha my Divine Healer and supernatural Health. This is what Abba desires to do for you as well as you get revelation through this book concerning God's covenant promises from Holy Spirit.

Please remember that God's healing and health, God's prosperity and wealth, and God's success and victory is already included in our new life in Christ. So, walk in your complete redemption in Christ Jesus, our Lord Adonai, as we enjoy every Covenant Blessing included in "The Seven Redemptive Names of Christ Jesus, our Lord."

2 JEHOVAH SHAMMAH: GOD'S GLORY AND PRESENCE WITHIN US

JEHOVAH SHAMMAH IS one of the redemptive names of Jesus. Shammah means "the Lord our God is eternally present in us and with us." He surrounds the New Covenant believer with His heavenly presence; His anointing dwells within us. We are in the glory realm, and His Shekinah Glory dwells inside of us eternally. He will never leave us or forsake us. His indwelling presence heals and keeps us whole.

Every born-again believer is the eternal dwelling place of Jehovah Shammah because the Godhead (Father, Son, and Holy Spirit) lives in us right now through our redemption.

As far back as I can remember, I battled a spirit of fear, which pushed me into a desperate search for God. This spirit of fear caused me a lot of emotional dysfunction which resulted in causing me to develop many phobias. I can often remember laying in my bed at night asking God to please help me to go to sleep. I would often feel His presence; this would calm me down and the next thing I remember, it would be morning.

As I grew stronger in the Lord, Holy Spirit began to reveal Christ to me as Jehovah Shammah. He taught me that He was the greater one who dwells within me and that He did not give me the spirit of fear, but that He would teach me through these scriptures that He gave me the spirit of power, His love and a sound and well-balanced mind. Holy Spirit taught me that the God head lives within us to heal, deliver and make us whole, spirit, soul and body.

We are God's temple and His executive orders to His Church is that "we bring glory and honor to Him in our bodies." I invite you to receive some awesome revelations from each one of the scriptures in this chapter that will reveal Jehovah Shammah, the Lord our God, who is eternally present in us and with us.

Once I understood from the Word of God that the power and authority of God's spirit lives in me. I began to stand in faith for every covenant promise of God. I began to believe that first, I am never alone, the spirit of God dwells in me and second, that it is His glorious power that heals me. Holy Spirit gave me some more powerful revelations from our next scripture.

> *Colossians 2:9-10 (AMP)*
>
> *9 For in Him the whole fullness of Deity (the Godhead) continues to dwell in bodily form [giving complete expression of the divine nature].*
>
> *10 And you are in Him, made full and having come to fullness of life [in Christ you too are filled with the Godhead—Father, Son and Holy Spirit—and reach full spiritual stature]. And He is the Head of all rule and authority [of every angelic principality and power].*

Holy Spirit was responsible for the resurrection of Christ Jesus from the dead. He is the same Spirit that restores our physical bodies to divine health. Every day He desires to quicken us which means, "to make us well, to revive us and bring our bodies into order and wholeness." He permeates our bodies daily with God's spirit life. I learned from the Word of God that Christ Jesus is our personal physician and I don't have to be afraid of the devil's lies anymore!

Verse 9: The fullness of the Godhead continues to dwell in the immortal body of Christ Jesus even today. As Christ is right now in heaven, so are we right now on earth.

Verse 10: Every born-again believer has the Lord's eternal life in our re-born spirits. Our spirit man is heaven ready right now. We also have the Lord's (zoé) spirit life in us through the quickening power of the Holy Spirit flowing through our physical bodies bringing healing and divine health to all our flesh daily.

> *Romans 8:11 (AMP)*
>
> *11 And if the Spirit of Him Who raised up Jesus from the dead dwells in you, [then] He Who raised up Christ Jesus from the dead will also restore to life your mortal (short-lived, perishable) bodies through His Spirit Who dwells in you.*

Repeat this with me: "Jehovah Shammah's presence lives in me right now! In Jesus Name! I have the Healer living in me!"

Let's go to another scripture that helped to strengthen my faith and bought me to some great deliverances and became the foundational scripture for the vision of our church, Full Gospel Foundation Building Ministries International. The scriptures taught me how the God head is used to bring us into purpose.

Ephesians 2:19-22 (AMP)

19 Therefore you are no longer outsiders (exiles, migrants, and aliens, excluded from the rights of citizens), but you now share citizenship with the saints (God's own people, consecrated and set apart for Himself); and you belong to God's [own] household.

20 You are built upon the foundation of the apostles and prophets with Christ Jesus Himself the chief Cornerstone.

21 In Him the whole structure is joined (bound, welded) together harmoniously, and it continues to rise (grow, increase) into a holy temple in the Lord [a sanctuary dedicated, consecrated, and sacred to the presence of the Lord].

22 In Him [and in fellowship with one another] you yourselves also are being built up [into this

> *structure] with the rest, to form a fixed abode (dwelling place) of God in (by, through) the Spirit.*

I know now that I am a righteous citizen of God's kingdom, the dwelling place of my creator I learned from this scripture in verses 19-20 that every born-again believer is a citizen of God's Kingdom and a member of God's royal family. The foundational teachings of God's Apostles and Prophets continually build us up. The chief cornerstone of what God is building is Christ Jesus Himself.

Verses 21-22: Every believer is God's Holy Temple, His sanctuary. We are joined together to reveal Jehovah Shammah, God's supernatural presence to this world. We are God's eternal dwelling place through Holy Spirit.

> *Ephesians 3:16-21 (AMP)*
>
> *16 May He grant you out of the rich treasury of His glory to be strengthened and reinforced with mighty power in the inner man by the [Holy] Spirit [Himself indwelling your innermost being and personality].*
>
> *17 May Christ through your faith [actually] dwell (settle down, abide, make His permanent home) in your hearts! May you be rooted deep in love and founded securely on love,*

18 That you may have the power and be strong to apprehend and grasp with all the saints [God's devoted people, the experience of that love] what is the breadth and length and height and depth [of it];

19 [That you may really come] to know [practically, through experience for yourselves] the love of Christ, which far surpasses mere knowledge [without experience]; that you may be filled [through all your being] unto all the fullness of God [may have the richest measure of the divine Presence, and become a body wholly filled and flooded with God Himself]!

20 Now to Him Who, by (in consequence of) the [action of His] power that is at work within us, is able to [carry out His purpose and] do superabundantly, far over and above all that we [dare] ask or think [infinitely beyond our highest prayers, desires, thoughts, hopes, or dreams]—

21 To Him be glory in the church and in Christ Jesus throughout all generations forever and ever. Amen (so be it).

Within these powerful scriptures get ready to experience how Jehovah Shammah's supernatural presence is working in every new covenant believer so we can learn how to cooperate with the Godhead daily.

Verse 16: First, we can see how **Holy Spirit**, Himself dwells in our inner man and personality. As we submit to Him, He will develop the fruit of our new nature according to Galatians 5:22-23 (AMP).

> *Galatians 5:22-23 (AMP)*
>
> *22 But the fruit of the [Holy] Spirit [the work which His presence within accomplishes] is love, joy (gladness), peace, patience (an even temper, forbearance), kindness, goodness (benevolence), faithfulness,*
>
> *23 Gentleness (meekness, humility), self-control (self-restraint, continence). Against such things there is no law [[a]that can bring a charge].*

Holy Spirit is also in us to strengthen and reinforce God's (dunamis) mighty power in us through our Faith in Christ Jesus. Faith requires our positive response to God's Word. *Ephesians 3:17-18:* Second, we can see how **Christ Jesus** is dwelling permanently in our re-born spirits, so by releasing our faith in Him we can experience God's hesed—agape, unconditional love every day. It is the power of Christ in us that will cause God's love to be rooted deep in our hearts so we can experience it daily. Remember Christ first loved us and gave His life for us, now we can love others with God's love in us.

THE SEVEN REDEMPTIVE NAMES OF CHRIST JESUS

Verse 19: Next, we can see how **God the Father, Himself**, calls every believer to be wholly filled and flooded with "the zóé life and power" that comes from Jehovah Shammah Himself, the Godhead is ever present within us. This is all possible because of the Finished works of Calvary's cross. One God in three persons.

Verse 20: God's (dunamis), His creative, immeasurable, unlimited and surpassing power is at work in every born-again believer in Christ Jesus so we can fulfill God's divine purpose for our lives here on earth healthy and whole. God has given every believer *His* authority (exousia), *His* ability (kratos) and *His* powerful might (dunamis).

Jehovah Shammah, our ever-present God lives in us and it is He that qualifies and is able to do exceedingly and super abundantly above all, (anything) that we would dare ask for in prayer or in our faith confessions or what we can think through our renewed minds.

Ephesians 1:4-5 (AMP)

4 Even as [in His love] He chose us [actually picked us out for Himself as His own] in Christ before the foundation of the world, that we should be holy (consecrated and set apart for Him) and blameless in His sight, even above reproach, before Him in love.

> *5 For He foreordained us (destined us, planned in love for us) to be adopted (revealed) as His own children through Jesus Christ, in accordance with the purpose of His will [[because it pleased Him and was His kind intent]—*

Christ Jesus chose us and adopted us as His dwelling place before the foundation of the world because it pleased Him to love those of us in Christ. All we have to do is accept Jesus as our personal Savior and Lord and He moves inside of us with all His glorious presence, authority and power.

Ephesians 3:21: Because of Jehovah Shammah's divine presence within every new covenant believer, we are empowered to give the Godhead glory (doxa) which means the highest honor in the Lord's Church through every generation forever and ever. For many years during my early walk with Christ, I would often wonder, "Where is God?" I did not feel Him, I would ask, "Did you leave me, did I grieve you?" I didn't understand that through God's abundant grace—His unearned, undeserved and unmerited favor—I am His eternal dwelling place all because Jehovah Shammah is our ever-present God through the finished works of Calvary's Cross. I had to learn how to believe this truth.

I now understand that Jehovah Shammah dwells in me. I can now rest in Him because He will never leave me or forsake me. He is our ever-present God, Jehovah Shammah. I have an intimacy with Him as I worship Him daily. My worship and praise bring His Glory realm within me wherever I go.

As Jehovah Shammah, our Redeemer, we now have His manifested presence living in us forever. Walk in His glorious presence every day because where the presence of the Lord is there is liberty from all sickness and diseases through our precious Holy Spirit, who dwells inside of every New Covenant believer.

3 JEHOVAH SHALOM: GOD'S PEACE AND WELL-BEING

THE NEXT REDEMPTIVE name of Christ Jesus is Jehovah Shalom. He is our Prince of Peace and wellbeing. Peace is a person, the Lord Jesus Christ.

Peace is a spiritual force that dwells on the inside of every born-again believer. There can be chaos all around us but because of the Spirit of Christ Jesus dwelling inside of our born-again spirit, we have inherited a position of Peace. There will be nothing missing, nothing broken and nothing lacking in our lives. God's Peace is a part of our new divine nature.

I revealed in a previous chapter that I experienced a lot of trauma in my teenaged years which caused me to experience many severe outbreaks of eczema that would cover my entire body. I would try to hide my body all the time as this condition caused me to have a lot of stress and anxiety.

I grew up in a housing project living with both my parents, my sister and five of my brothers. My dad was never home on the weekends. He would leave home on Friday evenings and I would not see him again until Monday mornings before I went to school. I don't have to tell you how angry, fearful and abandoned I felt all those years. His absence caused me to develop a spirit of depression and rejection that released emotional reaction in my life. These negative feelings triggered chemical imbalances, which caused my skin to break out year after year along with panic attacks that led me to many phobias.

After many years of this negative behavior, one day I cried out to God for his help and Holy Spirit began to speak to me about my emotions being the trigger for these demonic attacks in my life. Holy Spirit began to give me revelation about how to fix my toxic emotion. He began to teach me about God's spiritual force of inner peace that came to live in me at the time of my born-again experience. Then Holy Spirit taught me that God's peace is a part of our new divine nature revealed in Galatians 5:22-23 (AMP).

> *Galatians 5:22-23 (AMP)*
>
> *22 But the fruit of the [Holy] Spirit [the work which His presence within accomplishes] is love, joy (gladness), peace, patience (an even temper, forbearance), kindness, goodness (benevolence), faithfulness,*
>
> *23 Gentleness (meekness, humility), self-control (self-restraint, continence). Against such things there is no law [that can bring a charge].*

Holy Spirit also revealed to me that there was a divine exchange made through the redemptive work of Calvary's Cross. The Blood of Jesus purchased our Shalom Peace which means wholeness, wellness, wellbeing, divine health, completeness, prosperity and wealth.

Let's begin building our foundation from an Old Testament scripture that is vitally important to every new covenant believer's life because it reveals Jehovah Shalom, our Peace.

Isaiah 53:4-5 (AMP)

4 Surely He has borne our griefs (sicknesses, weaknesses, and distresses) and carried our sorrows and pains [of punishment], yet we [ignorantly] considered Him stricken, smitten, and afflicted by God [as if with leprosy].

5 But He was wounded for our transgressions, He was bruised for our guilt and iniquities; the chastisement [needful to obtain] peace and well-being for us was upon Him, and with the stripes [that wounded] Him we are healed and made whole.

Verse 4: The word *griefs* in the Hebrew is translated sicknesses, weaknesses and distresses. This speaks to every spiritual, physical, mental problem, that we would experience in life. I want to share with you how this powerful scripture changed my life forever.

Spiritually, I began to study the Word of God daily. I learned that God's spirit and His faith substance dwells in my spirit to keep me healthy and whole. I began walking around making faith confessions until I could understand how important meditating on God's Word would cause His word to become flesh to me. I also learned that my soul was made up of three parts that I had to learn to manage properly. Our mind is our thinker, our will is our chooser and our emotions are our feeler.

THE SEVEN REDEMPTIVE NAMES OF CHRIST JESUS

My emotions were being influenced by many demonic fears and anxiety attacks which effected my physical health. I began to understand that within my new nature is the Spirit of Peace. I had to allow Holy Spirit to reveal to me that Jesus carried every one of our sorrows and pains of punishments on Calvary's cross. Everything you and I should be punished for, God put it on Jesus; He bore it for us and purchased our righteousness in Christ through his precious blood.

Verse 5: Because of God's abundant gift of Grace every one of our sins: past, present and future were forgiven on Calvary's Cross. Holy Spirit put our complete redemption in the past tense, so should we.

Jesus was also crushed for our guilt and iniquities, the root of our old sin nature. This is also referring to every generational curse or sins that were passed down through our parents' DNA. Not one curse has a legal right to come against a New Covenant believer because Jesus, our Prince of Peace became the curse of the law for us according to Galatians 3:13-14.

Galatians 3:13-14 (AMP)

13 Christ purchased our freedom [redeeming us] from the curse (doom) of the Law [and its condemnation] by [Himself] becoming a curse for us, for it is

> written [in the Scriptures], Cursed is everyone who
> hangs on a tree (is crucified);
>
> [14] To the end that through [their receiving] Christ
> Jesus, the blessing [promised] to Abraham might
> come upon the Gentiles, so that we through faith
> might [all] receive [the realization of] the promise of
> the [Holy] Spirit.

Also, in Isaiah 53:5 the scripture states that "the punishment" that we deserved was put on Christ Jesus so that we could inherit His Peace (Shalom) and well-being (health and wholeness). His punishment brought our peace.

In the courts of heaven, a believer cannot be punished twice for the same crime, this would be called double jeopardy. Jesus was punished for our sins and sicknesses on the cross of Calvary. He did not just die *for us*, but Jesus died *as us*. So, we do not have to be punished for them because our heavenly Father recognizes that we died with Christ, was buried with Him and when He rose from the dead, we rose with Him. (read Roman 6:3-11) This is called God's Grace. His underserved, unearned, and unmerited favor. The moment you and I were forgiven, we were also healed of all sicknesses and diseases under the curse because all of the curse was the results of sin; we were forgiven; therefore, we were also healed!

THE SEVEN REDEMPTIVE NAMES OF CHRIST JESUS

These next two scriptures were given to me by Holy Spirit when I was at one of the lowest places in my life. At times I would only be able to sleep for maybe one or two hours a night. The rest of the night I would experience the torment of itching and burning of my skin. Some nights I would find myself crying all night and begging God to help me to sleep. Often, I would walk around all day drained and tired. My five senses were controlling my emotions until Holy Spirit taught me that I had received my new emotions according to Galatians 5:22-23 which included the Spirit of Peace.

I began playing healing tapes over and over every day until one day I heard a faith teacher say, "The reason you have no peace is because you believe your disease is taking over" and that day I got my deliverance. I repented before God and admitted to Him that I was allowing fear and unbelief to control my emotions. I realized that I was quoting scriptures that declared that I was already healed but, in my heart, I was still waiting for the manifestation and this is not true faith, because faith is always now! Let's now go to John 14:25-27 (AMP).

John 14:25-27 (AMP)

25 I have told you these things while I am still with you.

*26 But the Comforter (Counselor, Helper, Interces-
sor, Advocate, Strengthener, Standby), the Holy
Spirit, Whom the Father will send in My name [in
My place, to represent Me and act on My behalf],
He will teach you all things. And He will cause you
to recall (will remind you of, bring to your remembrance) everything I have told you.*

*27 Peace I leave with you; My [own] peace I now
give and bequeath to you. Not as the world gives do
I give to you. Do not let your hearts be troubled,
neither let them be afraid. [Stop allowing yourselves
to be agitated and disturbed; and do not permit
yourselves to be fearful and intimidated and cowardly and unsettled.]*

I would like to share with you what Holy Spirit has
taught me in these three verses:

Verse 26: These are attributes and characteristics of
the promised Holy Spirit available to every new covenant
believer because of Jehovah Shalom's Peace dwelling
inside of us.

Verse 27: Jesus left His Peace (Shalom) with His
Church, He has bequeathed it, this means to give or pass
on to another; He gave His Peace to every believer. Peace
is the grace gift of God. His favor is not earned or
deserved; it is the gift of God to His Church. Jesus has
overcome this world for us.

THE SEVEN REDEMPTIVE NAMES OF CHRIST JESUS

I heard the Holy Spirit personally say to me that, "Jesus said to stop tolerating the devil's deceptions, He is already defeated and sentenced." Christ Jesus revealed this truth to the church in John 16:11 (AMP).

> *John 16:11 (AMP)*
>
> *11 About judgment, because the ruler (evil genius, prince) of this world [Satan] is judged and condemned and sentence already is passed upon him.*

I realized once revelation came to me that Satan was not my problem, fear was not my problem, and neither was eczema or any of the other phobias that I had been experiencing. It is because of the blood of Calvary's cross that Jesus declared it is finished!

The scripture says that in the mouth of two or three witness let every word be established. So, let's go to this next scripture that also gave me great faith in Jehovah Shalom, John 16:33 (AMP).

> *John 16:33 (AMP)*
>
> *33 I have told you these things, so that in Me you may have [perfect] peace and confidence. In the world you have tribulation and trials and distress and frustration; but be of good cheer [take courage; be confident, certain, undaunted]! For I have*

overcome the world. [I have deprived it of power to harm you and have conquered it for you.]

Jesus declares that "I have told you things about my perfect peace before, Jesus talks about having perfect Peace and confidence" in Him. He lets us know that we will have troubles in this world, but we must remember that we are in this world, but we are not of this world, so keep your focus on him and start declaring Ephesians 2:6 (AMP).

Ephesians 2:6 (AMP)

6 And He raised us up together with Him and made us sit down together [giving us joint seating with Him] in the heavenly sphere [by virtue of our being] in Christ Jesus (the Messiah, the Anointed One).

Church, because we are seated far above the works of the devil, we should not allow ourselves to be troubled, afraid, agitated by the devil, disturbed or fearful, intimidated, act cowardly and unsettled because through the finished works of Calvary's Cross, Jesus has overcome the world. This world has no power over us, so be of good cheer, take courage and be confident because Jehovah Shalom (the Prince of Peace) dwells in every believer.

So, let's get revelation from this final scripture in John 15:7-8 (AMP).

> *John 15:7-8 (AMP)*
>
> *7 If you live in Me [abide vitally united to Me] and My words remain in you and continue to live in your hearts, ask whatever you will, and it shall be done for you.*
>
> *8 When you bear (produce) much fruit, My Father is honored and glorified, and you show and prove yourselves to be true followers of Mine.*

This powerful scripture gives us the prerequisite for producing much fruit which I call manifestation. The scriptures reveal that we are to bring honor and glory to our Heavenly Father by abiding in Christ and allowing His Word to remain in our hearts then we can command from our righteous position in Christ whatever his covenant promises are. Jesus said it shall be done for us. So, we can begin every new day declaring Peace, Peace! Jesus said, "My Peace—My Shalom, I leave with you." Allow the Holy Spirit to operate in you through Christ Jesus, our Jehovah Shalom, in every situation that you will face in this life.

APOSTLE CHERYL FORTSON

Remember, just as Jehovah Shalom, our Redeemer, we now have His indwelling peace and wellbeing! Walk in His Shalom Peace every day.

4 JEHOVAH ROHI: GOD'S CHIEF SHEPHERD AND PROTECTOR

T HE NEXT REDEMPTIVE name of Christ Jesus is Jehovah Rohi. This name means that Jesus is the Chief Shepherd of His new covenant church. Our great Shepherd laid down His life for His sheep in order to give us life and life more abundant.

In the early days of the patriarchs, shepherding was a prosperous occupation. It was the shepherd that guided the sheep, he was the caretaker of the flock.

Many years ago, I was sent by God to minister out of state. One night after I returned to my hotel room the Holy Spirit led me to Ezekiel 34. These scriptures taught me about God's definition of false shepherds. The spirit of God also revealed to me that there are spiritual leaders whom God said that destruction would be certain for them because they were feeding themselves instead of their flock. Scripture also reveals that they were not taking care of the sheep that were weak, nor were they tending to the sheep that were sick or going after those that had wandered away. God revealed to me that these false shepherds were ruling the sheep with force and cruelty causing them to be easy prey for the enemy. The Lord considered these shepherds to be His enemies and declared in the Word that He would hold them responsible for what was happening to his flock. So, the Lord declared to me that He would rescue His flock from these false shepherds and bring them home to their own land from exile.

The spirit of God on that night revealed to me the heart of our Father towards His sheep. On that night in my hotel room I began to cry, and I was immediately reminded by the spirit of God that this was why Jesus came to earth, moved with pity and compassion for His sheep that were without true shepherds in this world. He showed to me in the New Testament that we were to pray for laborers to bring in the harvest.

It would be several years later that I would hear the call of God on my life to become one of His undershepherds and I then remembered my visitation with the Lord that night in that hotel room when he gave me revelation from Ezekiel chapter 34.

The Hebrew word for shepherd is also translated "feeding." The shepherd also led the sheep to pasture and water protected them from danger.

Let's receive some important revelations from an Old Testament Psalm that reveals the true Shepherd, God's Covenant promise of Jehovah Rohi, who is Christ Jesus, our Lord.

Psalm 23 (AMP)

1 The Lord is my Shepherd [to feed, guide, and shield me], I shall not lack.

2 He makes me lie down in [fresh, tender] green pastures; He leads me beside the still and restful waters.

3 He refreshes and restores my life (myself); He leads me in the paths of righteousness [uprightness and right standing with Him—not for my earning it, but] for His name's sake.

4 Yes, though I walk through the [deep, sunless] valley of the shadow of death, I will fear or dread no evil, for You are with me; Your rod [to protect] and Your staff [to guide], they comfort me.

5 You prepare a table before me in the presence of my enemies. You anoint my head with oil; my [brimming] cup runs over.

6 Surely or only goodness, mercy, and unfailing love shall follow me all the days of my life, and through the length of my days the house of the Lord [and His presence] shall be my dwelling place.

This psalm will take us from God's Old Testament Promise of Jehovah Rohi to His fulfillment of our Chief Shepherd in the New Covenant.

Verse 1: This is a redemptive promise from God that our Chief Shepherd, Christ Jesus, will provide these three vital things for His sheep "to feed, to guide and shield us."

Our chief Shepherd has promised that His sheep shall not lack; His sheep will have everything they need. We are His sheep, and He promised there will be nothing missing, broken or lacking in our lives because of our Good Shepherd. Let's go to John 10:11-15; 27-29 for more revelation concerning our good shepherd.

John 10:11-15; 27-29 (AMP)

11 I am the Good Shepherd. The Good Shepherd risks and lays down His [own] life for the sheep.

12 But the hired servant (he who merely serves for wages) who is neither the shepherd nor the owner of the sheep, when he sees the wolf coming, deserts the flock and runs away. And the wolf chases and snatches them and scatters [the flock].

13 Now the hireling flees because he merely serves for wages and is not himself concerned about the sheep [cares nothing for them].

14 I am the Good Shepherd; and I know and recognize My own, and My own know and recognize Me—

15 Even as [truly as] the Father knows Me and I also know the Father—and I am giving My [very own] life and laying it down on behalf of the sheep.

27 The sheep that are My own hear and are listening to My voice; and I know them, and they follow Me.

28 And I give them eternal life, and they shall never lose it or perish throughout the ages. [To all eternity they shall never by any means be destroyed.] And no one is able to snatch them out of My hand.

29 My Father, Who has given them to Me, is greater and mightier than all [else]; and no one is able to snatch [them] out of the Father's hand.

These verses in John 10 gave me the security I really needed to overcome my fears. Let's go back to our foundation scripture in Psalm 23 and receive more revelation from Holy Spirit about Jehovah Rohi.

Psalm 23, Verse 2: Our Chief Shepherd promises as Jehovah Rohi that He will provide us with His "Sabboth Rest" every day of our lives. These New Testament scriptures gave me an awesome revelation about God's covenant promise about rest.

Let's go to Hebrews 4:1-11 (AMP). *Read in message*

Hebrews 4:1-11 (AMP)

1 Therefore, while the promise of entering His rest still holds and is offered [today], let us be afraid [to distrust it], lest any of you should think he has come too late and has come short of [reaching] it.

2 For indeed we have had the glad tidings [Gospel of God] proclaimed to us just as truly as they [the Israelites of old did when the good news of deliverance from bondage came to them]; but the message they heard did not benefit them, because it was not mixed with faith (with the leaning of the entire personality on God in absolute trust and confidence in His power, wisdom, and goodness) by those who heard it; neither were they united in faith with the ones [Joshua and Caleb] who heard (did believe).

Glad in Passion

3 For we who have believed (adhered to and trusted in and relied on God) do enter that rest, in accordance with His declaration that those [who did not believe] should not enter when He said, As I swore in My wrath, They shall not enter My rest; and this He said although [His] works had been completed and prepared [and waiting for all who would believe] from the foundation of the world.

4 For in a certain place He has said this about the seventh day: And God rested on the seventh day from all His works.

5 And [they forfeited their part in it, for] in this [passage] He said, They shall not enter My rest.

6 Seeing then that the promise remains over [from past times] for some to enter that rest, and that those who formerly were given the good news about it and the opportunity, failed to appropriate it and did not enter because of disobedience,

7 Again He sets a definite day, [a new] Today, [and gives another opportunity of securing that rest] saying through David after so long a time in the words already quoted, Today, if you would hear His voice and when you hear it, do not harden your hearts.

8 [This mention of a rest was not a reference to their entering into Canaan.] For if Joshua had given them rest, He [God] would not speak afterward about another day.

9 So then, there is still awaiting a full and complete Sabbath-rest reserved for the [true] people of God;

10 For he who has once entered [God's] rest also has ceased from [the weariness and pain] of human labors, just as God rested from those labors [peculiarly His own.

11 Let us therefore be zealous and exert ourselves and strive diligently to enter that rest [of God, to know and experience it for ourselves], that no one may fall or perish by the same kind of unbelief and disobedience [into which those in the wilderness fell].

This executive order from Christ Jesus instructs His Church to strive diligently to rest in him. This order was not very easy for me to do because of all the different fleshly fears that I was warring against. I often struggled to rest in the Lord. Praise God, I began to learn from the Word of God that this Sabboth rest for the New Covenant believer is called Jesus. We are summoned to rest in the fearless, flawless faith of Christ Jesus. Jesus, our Chief Shepherd, has successfully completed His works for us from the foundation of the World. When he was originally slain for us before entering the world.

Our Chief Shepherd is declaring His Rest because He said, "I have completed your salvation; I have given you rest from toil." The only time He told us to labor was to labor to enter into His rest (rest does not mean inactivity; we work from the place of finished). We are to stop all self-effort which are the works of the flesh. Our Chief Shepherd protects us from all of our enemies, and this is something that I had to learn to believe. We must renew our minds with the Word of God because the Lord's works have been finished from before the foundation of the world, and because of His indwelling Holy Spirit living within us, we have rivers of living water flowing in us, and through us in order to set the captives free. Our Chief Shepherd promised this blessing to every new covenant believer revealed in John 7:37-39 (AMP).

John 7:37-39 (AMP)

37 Now on the final and most important day of the Feast, Jesus stood, and He cried in a loud voice, If any man is thirsty, let him come to Me and drink!

38 He who believes in Me [who cleaves to and trusts in and relies on Me] as the Scripture has said, From his innermost being shall flow [continuously] springs and rivers of living water.

> *39 But He was speaking here of the Spirit, Whom those who believed (trusted, had faith) in Him were afterward to receive. For the [Holy] Spirit had not yet been given, because Jesus was not yet glorified (raised to honor).*

Let's go back to our foundation scripture in Psalm 23, verse 3. Our Chief Shepherd promises to refresh and restore our life and to bring us back to health and wholeness, completeness and soundness. This is already ours in Christ Jesus; He is our Sabboth Rest.

As New Covenant believers we must learn how to operate in "the realm of the Finished." Which means that I had to learn how to believe from the Word of God that every covenant blessing has been purchased and paid for in full by the precious blood of Christ Jesus. For every new covenant believer Jesus fulfilled the entire curse that began in Garden of Eden and has now qualifies us to operate in the realm called finished. Ephesians 1:3 declares that God has blessed us in Christ with every spiritual blessing in the heavenly realm which is also called the realm of the finished or the supernatural causal realms. All of God's covenant blessings will be given to us by Holy Spirit through faith in the finished works of Calvary's cross because these blessings already belong to us in Christ Jesus.

Our chief Shepherd leads us in the paths of righteousness, so we can bring honor to His precious Name.

Righteousness for the new covenant believer is a "gift" from our great shepherd. We cannot earn it, nor did we do anything to deserve it, Christ Jesus qualified us according to scripture in Romans 5:17.

Romans 5:17 (AMP)

17 For if because of one man's trespass (lapse, offense) death reigned through that one, much more surely will those who receive [God's] overflowing grace (unmerited favor) and the free gift of righteousness [putting them into right standing with Himself] reign as kings in life through the one Man Jesus Christ (the Messiah, the Anointed One).

Because of our Savior's s overflowing grace, His unmerited favor, every believer has received at the new birth our Lord's Righteousness, right standing with Him and a Kingly anointing given to us so that we can legislate, dominate, rule and reign here on earth through Christ Jesus our Lord. Holy Spirit reminded me that kings don't ask or beg! Righteousness is God's Grace Gift to everyone that our good shepherd died for.

Psalm 23 verse 4: Jehovah Rohi reveals to us that in this life we will go through trials and tribulations, but we are not to fear or dread the illegal attacks of our enemies. Our Chief Shepherd will never leave us or forsake us. His rod of protection and His staff of guidance will comfort us all the days of our life.

One of the most destructive phobias that I experienced in my youth was the fear of death and at the same time I also feared life. There was a void in my life because I felt so alone and suffered from a spirit of desertion. I was in desperate need of my heavenly Father's protection. I would always tell God that I loved Him, but I knew very little about His unconditional love for me until I found out in scripture that my good shepherd loved me so much that He died for me. I also found out when the Holy Spirit led me to 2 Timothy 1:7 that He didn't give me the spirit of fear.

II Timothy 1:7 (AMP)

7 For God did not give us a spirit of timidity (of cowardice, of craven and cringing and fawning fear), but [He has given us a spirit] of power and of love and of calm and well-balanced mind and discipline and self-control.

Our Chief Shepherd gave these three covenants promises to every New Covenant believer:

THE SEVEN REDEMPTIVE NAMES OF CHRIST JESUS

1. A spirit of power – This is His dunamis might and strength that causes us to defeat all the evils of this life.
2. He gave us his Hesed agape love – This means His unconditional, unchangeable Love.
3. He gave us a sound, well-balanced mind, which has given us the mind of Christ.

Also, in *Psalm 23 verse 4,* He promises us that the Lord's rod and staff will comfort us all the days of our life. This promises us that God's eternal Word will guide us, protect us and comfort us during every test and trial. I had to learn to believe this in order to feel secure in Christ.

Let's go back *Psalm 23 verse 5.* Our Chief Shepherd promises to prepare a table before us right in the presence of our enemy and to anoint our heads with oil until our cup runs over.

I received one of the most life-changing revelations from Holy Spirit concerning the table that our Chief Shepherd has prepared for His New Covenant church for us in the presence of our enemies.

This table literally helped God to save my life and I now want to share what Holy Spirit revealed to me.

I Corinthians 11:23-30 (AMP)

23 For I received from the Lord Himself that which I passed on to you [it was given to me personally], that the Lord Jesus on the night when He was treacherously delivered up and while His betrayal was in progress took bread,

24 And when He had given thanks, He broke [it] and said, Take, eat. This is My body, which is broken for you. Do this to call Me [affectionately] to remembrance.

25 Similarly when supper was ended, He took the cup also, saying, This cup is the new covenant [ratified and established] in My blood. Do this, as often as you drink [it], to call Me [affectionately] to remembrance.

26 For every time you eat this bread and drink this cup, you are representing and signifying and proclaiming the fact of the Lord's death until He comes [again].

27 So then whoever eats the bread or drinks the cup of the Lord in a way that is unworthy [of Him] will be guilty of [profaning and sinning against] the body and blood of the Lord.

28 Let a man [thoroughly] examine himself, and [only when he has done] so should he eat of the bread and drink of the cup.

29 For anyone who eats and drinks without discriminating and recognizing with due appreciation that [it is Christ's] body, eats and drinks a sentence (a verdict of judgment) upon himself.

30 That [careless and unworthy participation] is the reason many of you are weak and sickly, and quite enough of you have fallen into the sleep of death.

This is the meal that reminds us every day that we have a complete redemption from the entire curse that began in the Garden of Eden after the fall of man. This meal proclaims that proof of the finished work of Calvary's Cross.

The bread represents the Lord's body; beaten, bruised, broken and striped for all our sicknesses and diseases. The cup represents the Lord's blood shed for the forgiveness of all our sins. It was His wounds that forgave us of all our past, present and future sins and has made the New Covenant believer eternally righteous. We are in right standing with God forever.

Let's get revelation from Holy Spirit in verse 27, This scripture uses the words "unworthy of Him" which means that by not understanding that this meal is not only natural elements but is the Lord's body and His blood, we are not honoring His finished work on Calvary's cross. We must get understanding about what His body and His blood did for us on Calvary's Cross when we eat and drink this meal.

Verse 28: We are commanded to properly "examine ourselves" before we eat and drink which means to thoroughly understand that His body was already striped for us and has already healed us. His blood was already shed for us and has forgiven us and declared us eternally righteous forever through the Lord's finished works of Calvary's cross.

Verse 29: We are also commanded to discern, which means to discriminate, to recognize with due appreciation, to perceive and to have a clear understanding that the bread is the body of Christ Jesus and the cup is the blood of Christ Jesus. When we fail to obey the Lord's executive orders concerning the Holy Communion meal God's verdict and sentence of judgement is revealed in verse 30. When we don't have the right revelation of the Lord's sacrifice on Calvary's cross, there are three things mentioned in this verse that will happen to believers in the church.

Verse 30: Failure to properly discern is considered careless and unworthy participation when partaking of the Lord's table that our Good Shepherd prepares for us in the presence of our enemies.

THE SEVEN REDEMPTIVE NAMES OF CHRIST JESUS

This Scripture in *(verse 30)* reveals the reason that many in the body of Christ are weak instead of strong and sickly instead of healthy and whole and dying prematurely instead of living a long prosperous life that was promised to us in Christ Jesus because of the finished work of Calvary's cross.

As we return to our last verse in Psalms 23:6, this scripture reveals God's covenant promise that His mercy and grace shall follow New Covenant believers all the days of our lives. Saints, mercy and grace is the person of Christ Jesus our Savior and Lord. He promises us also that Jehovah Shammah's glorious presence will live in us because we are the eternal dwelling place of the Lord. Jesus as Jehovah Rohi, our Chief Shepherd promises to feed us His word, to guides us in our divine purpose in this world and to shield and protect us from all evil, as we dwell in His presence forever.

Let's close this chapter in the revelation that taught me how to walk in great success through every test and trial that I will go through in this life. Jesus said in John 15:4-8 (AMP).

John 15:4-8 (AMP)

4 Dwell in Me, and I will dwell in you. [Live in Me, and I will live in you.] Just as no branch can bear fruit of itself without abiding in (being vitally united to) the vine, neither can you bear fruit unless you abide in Me.

5 I am the Vine; you are the branches. Whoever lives in Me and I in him bears much (abundant) fruit. However, apart from Me [cut off from vital union with Me] you can do nothing.

6 If a person does not dwell in Me, he is thrown out like a [broken-off] branch, and withers; such branches are gathered up and thrown into the fire, and they are burned.

7 If you live in Me [abide vitally united to Me] and My words remain in you and continue to live in your hearts, ask whatever you will, and it shall be done for you.

8 When you bear (produce) much fruit, My Father is honored and glorified, and you show and prove yourselves to be true followers of Mine.

We are the Lord's abiding branches revealed in John 15. We are full of God's Zoë (spirit life) and because of the finished works of Jehovah Rohi, our Chief Shepherd we will bear much abundant fruit as we bring glory and honor to our heavenly Father in our spirit, soul and body.

Just as Jehovah Rohi has redeemed us, we now have our Chief Shepherd's protection as we allow Him to shepherd us and protect us from all the evil attacks against our lives by the enemy. So, I charge you to walk in your freedom of divine health and wholeness every day!

5 JEHOVAH JIREH: GOD'S ETERNAL PROVIDER AND SOURCE

T HE NEXT REDEMPTIVE name of Christ Jesus, our Redeemer is Jehovah Jireh. This incredible name means, "I AM your eternal Provider that makes all things available to the new covenant believer."

Jehovah Jireh supplies all the necessities of life. He also comes into the believer's life to provide financial provisions, naturally and supernaturally. Jehovah Jireh keeps, maintains, supports and takes care of every need of the believer through His kingdom provisions, which includes God's divine healing and health.

Jesus truly became the source of my everything. This is when I began to know Him as my Jehovah Jireh. In 1987, the Lord informed me that He desired to begin the process of training me for full time ministry. What I found out after praying and asking God for understanding, He revealed to me that He was calling me from my job at the Hartford Insurance Company. God also revealed to me that He desired that I would volunteer in my church and start a ministry of visiting the sick and going into nursing homes to pray for people. Can you imagine what was going through my mind about not having a paycheck anymore, but most of all I had some concerns about what my husband was going to say about our family losing my income. I also was concerned about leaving the friends I worked with for many years. What would they think about my decision to leave the work force for ministry? This decision to trust God to become the source to meet my every need also included the fact that I would be giving up my retirement because I would be leaving two years before I would be vested.

I decided to help God out and quiet down my husband's emotions about just having one income coming into our house, and applying for a part-time job would serve both purposes (or so I thought). So, I went to Human

Resources to inquire about a part-time position and found out that one became available that very morning that I was qualified for. Even though this was not God's plan for me He helped me to obtain this position for eleven months because before I got home from the interview, they were calling me saying that I had gotten the position. Little did I know that my oldest son John, Jr. had talked to his father encouraging him to allow me to obey God's call on my life to prepare for full-time ministry.

I began my new part-time position, but my heart and mind were on ministry. I began to cry out to God to help me to get rid of the fear of leaving the corporate world and a paycheck. It was during this time God really began to introduce himself to me as Jehovah Jireh. After 11 months, I left that job to obey God and so many miraculous things began to happen that would teach me how to trust Jehovah Jireh to be my source. This scripture became rhema to me during those days.

Matthew 6:31-33 (AMP)

31 Therefore do not worry and be anxious, saying, What are we going to have to eat? or, What are we going to have to drink? or, What are we going to have to wear?

32 For the Gentiles (heathen) wish for and crave and diligently seek all these things, and your heavenly Father knows well that you need them all.

33 But seek (aim at and strive after) first of all His kingdom and His righteousness (His way of doing and being right), and then all these things [c]taken together will be given you besides.

I don't recommend that everyone who's called to ministry should leave their job, but this was God's direct instruction to *me*. I would find out several years later once I became the senior pastor of our church, why God's direction to me to trust Him to be my source was so important. God knew that I would need to know how to trust Him to meet my every need because there would be several years before I would be able to receive a salary from my church; thanks be to God I already knew how to trust God as the source of everything that I would need to pioneer Full Gospel Foundation Building Ministries International.

It was that experience and more that I believe qualifies me to share this revelation with you because I truly believe that Jehovah Jireh has promised every believer that when things look impossible God promises that He will always provide. Jehovah Jireh has commanded every believer not to worry or be anxious about our day-to-day needs.

THE SEVEN REDEMPTIVE NAMES OF CHRIST JESUS

The Gentiles, who didn't have a covenant with God, had to worry and be anxious. You and I serve a God who has finished everything for us before we would ever need it. Our inheritance is already provided for in the realm of the finished!

Jehovah Jireh became the miracle working God in my life. Two years after pioneering Full Gospel, God instructed me to begin looking for a building for our church home. We were renting space in a center as the church's membership continued to grow. We were informed by the owners of that center that they were very pleased with us because no other church that was renting from them were able to pay their rent a month ahead of time. I believed God every week for a specific amount of money to come in through our tithes and offerings and God blessed at every service so that we were able to take care of all our monthly needs on time. I have to admit that this was because I was taught by Holy Spirit all those years that He trained me for full-time ministry as my source.

I believe that before everything else in this life, we are commanded to keep our focus on God's Kingdom and righteousness. Everything you and I will ever need from God begins in His kingdom and it is vital that we understand our righteous identity in Christ Jesus.

Through a revelation from Holy Spirit in this next Old Testament scripture He revealed this powerful encounter to me concerning Father Abraham and how his faith was tested, and Jehovah Jireh was revealed to him because of his obedience to God. I learned how to trust God through many of my tests and trials because of the revelations I received in this Old Testament scripture. So, let's now read Genesis 22:1-14 (AMP).

Genesis 22:1-14 (AMP)

1 After these events, God tested and proved Abraham and said to him, Abraham! And he said, Here I am.

2 [God] said, Take now your son, your only son Isaac, whom you love, and go to the region of Moriah; and offer him there as a burnt offering upon one of the mountains of which I will tell you.

3 So Abraham rose early in the morning, saddled his donkey, and took two of his young men with him and his son Isaac; and he split the wood for the burnt offering, and then began the trip to the place of which God had told him.

4 On the third day Abraham looked up and saw the place in the distance.

5 And Abraham said to his servants, Settle down and stay here with the donkey, and I and the young man will go yonder and worship and come again to you.

6 Then Abraham took the wood for the burnt offering and laid it on [the shoulders of] Isaac his son, and he took the fire (the firepot) in his own hand, and a knife; and the two of them went on together.

7 And Isaac said to Abraham, My father! And he said, Here I am, my son. [Isaac] said, See, here are the fire and the wood, but where is the lamb for the burnt sacrifice?

8 Abraham said, My son, God Himself will provide a lamb for the burnt offering. So, the two went on together.

9 When they came to the place of which God had told him, Abraham built an altar there; then he laid the wood in order and bound Isaac his son and laid him on the altar on the wood.

10 And Abraham stretched forth his hand and took hold of the knife to slay his son.

11 But the Angel of the Lord called to him from heaven and said, Abraham, Abraham! He answered, Here I am.

12 And He said, Do not lay your hand on the lad or do anything to him; for now I know that you fear and revere God, since you have not held back from

> *Me or begrudged giving Me your son, your only son.*
>
> *13 Then Abraham looked up and glanced around, and behold, behind him was a ram caught in a thicket by his horns. And Abraham went and took the ram and offered it up for a burnt offering and an ascending sacrifice instead of his son!*
>
> *14 So Abraham called the name of that place The Lord Will Provide. And it is said to this day, On the mount of the Lord it will be provided.*

Holy Spirit revealed Father Abraham's faith to me in *verse 2* when God told Abraham to offer up his son who came from the supernatural intervention of God. Neither Abraham nor his barren wife could have a baby together at their old age, but God provided healing for both. Now Abraham's faith in God would be tested and proven because God asked him to sacrifice his miracle son.

In *verse 5*, Abraham's answer to God reveals that he believed that he and Isaac would be coming back down Mount Moriah together. Abraham remembered that God promised him that his son Isaac would inherit God's promise.

I learned the importance of speaking God's Word in every situation. Abraham believed God that he and his son, Isaac, was coming back down that mountain together so he declared it to his servants before he went up. I learned that Holy Spirit also needs our spoken word to perform our miracles that look impossible in the natural. So, I need you to remember that it is impossible for God to lie and all things are possible to those who believe Him. Remember our faith will not work until truth is known, Jesus is our truth!

Father Abraham remembered God's prophetic word to him, and this is why prophesy is so vitally important to every believer. I have learned to stand on my prophecy especially when I come under attack from the enemy and this is what Father Abraham remembered in Genesis 12:2-3 (AMP).

Genesis 12:2-3 (AMP)

2 And I will make of you a great nation, and I will bless you [with abundant increase of favors] and make your name famous and distinguished, and you will be a blessing [dispensing good to others].

3 And I will bless those who bless you [who confer prosperity or happiness upon you] and curse him who curses or uses insolent language toward you; in you will all the families and kindred of the earth be blessed [and by you they will bless themselves].

Let's go back to our foundation scripture in Genesis 22:7-8. Isaac understood, according to their culture, there was supposed to be a lamb for the sacrifice; so, where was it? Abraham spoke God's covenant provision out of his mouth, he said "God, Himself will provide a lamb." Abraham spoke prophetically, referring to Jesus, the Lamb of God who would take away the sin of the world.

I have also learned from Father Abraham how important it is to confess with my mouth every day that God is the source that meets my every need, because I now know Jesus as Jehovah Jireh my provider.

In *verse 9-12*, Abraham released his faith in God's Word and prepared to offer up Isaac when the Angel of the Lord (many scholars believe this was an appearance of Messiah), Israel's Savior appeared to him from heaven.

I also learned from Father Abraham that every born-again believer should desire a divine encounter with Christ Jesus as I did in January 1984. It was that encounter that changed my life forever. Before I ever think about giving up, I remember my Savior's prophetic words to me on that morning during my out of body experience with Him, how I looked at Him in all of His glory—I cannot give up because I know that even when I am faithless He remains faithful to me and He will do the same thing for you.

THE SEVEN REDEMPTIVE NAMES OF CHRIST JESUS

In *verse 13-14* God provided a sacrifice for Abraham's burnt offering instead of Isaac and Abraham called that place, "the Lord will provide, Jehovah Jireh."

Saints, I am positively persuaded that He will always provide whatever we need according to His riches in glory by Christ Jesus, our Lord. Let us now receive revelation from our new covenant about Jehovah Jireh, our Provider. It is important that we remember that God's Word promises His covenant people that "He would give us power to get or create wealth." Holy Spirit desires to teach us how to connect with Jehovah Jireh, our supernatural provider.

Let's go to a New Covenant scripture that has taught me how to trust the Lord every day as the true source that supplies my every need.

> *II Corinthians 9:8-11 (AMP)*
>
> *8 And God is able to make all grace (every favor and [earthly blessing) come to you in abundance, so that you may always and under all circumstances and whatever the need be self-sufficient [possessing enough to require no aid or support and furnished in abundance for every good work and charitable donation].*
>
> *9 As it is written, He [the benevolent person] scatters abroad; He gives to the poor; His deeds of*

*justice and goodness and kindness and benevolence
will go on and endure forever!*

*10 And [God] Who provides seed for the sower and
bread for eating will also provide and multiply your
[resources for] sowing and increase the fruits of
your righteousness [which manifests itself in active
goodness, kindness, and charity].*

*11 Thus you will be enriched in all things and in
every way, so that you can be generous, and [your
generosity as it is] administered by us will bring
forth thanksgiving to God.*

Here's the revelation from what Holy Spirit has taught me
in this powerful scripture. In *verse 8*, Jehovah Jireh ena-
bles every believer to operate in God's gift of Grace, His
favor and earthly blessing coming towards us in abundance. This scripture is in the present, active tense em-
powering us to prosper in our earthy purpose here on
earth continuously.

Verse 9: Because we are made in God's image and
likeness we are created to give, especially to the poor. We
must remember that we are not the poor, as long as the
earth remains there will be seed time and harvest time in
our lives. Our consistent giving will cause us to never
have a dry season. Our receiving will overtake our giving!

THE SEVEN REDEMPTIVE NAMES OF CHRIST JESUS

Verse 10-11: This is the key to allowing Jehovah Jireh to operate in our lives, we must make Him our source! This is the governmental order of God for releasing a harvest. There must be seed sown in order to release a harvest of the abundant blessings of Jehovah Jireh in our lives.

God promises that we will be "enriched," not just rich but wealthy and healthy because the Spirit of Jehovah Jireh dwells inside of every true believer in Christ Jesus.

I have also learned that we are commanded to prosper in every way, which also includes our physical bodies keeping well. There should be nothing missing, broken or lacking in our lives because God desires that our soul (mind, will and emotions) keeps well and prospers because Jehovah Jireh is the source of the believer's everything!

He provides the seed to sow, our bread to eat and He promises to increase our resources for sowing more for whatever we need.

As Jehovah Jireh, our Redeemer, we now have His eternal provisions to meet every need in our lives according to His riches in glory by Christ Jesus, our Lord.

Declare this Covenant Promise every day and walk in every Covenant benefit because Jesus is our eternal Provider. He not only provides our day-to-day natural needs, but the scripture reveals that Jehovah Jireh also provides this Covenant benefit: He heals us of all our diseases. So start walking today in God's divine provision by using your faith like Father Abraham, "calling for those things that be not as though they are and this is why because I now know that every covenant benefit from God has already been given to us by promise!" Let Jehovah Jireh be the source of your life.

6 JEHOVAH NISSI: GOD'S BANNER AND VICTOR

T HE NEXT REDEMPTIVE name of Christ Jesus is Jehovah Nissi. Nissi means Jehovah is our "Banner and Victor," which also means He is our protector and our triumphant warrior.

The Word "Banner" means "a flag, a standard, a pole, a rod and victory; the act of conquering, it also means to triumph, to win and master over." This name also reveals to the New Covenant believer that we should expect miracles through Jehovah Nissi. Things that look impossible are possible when you believe in our Lord, Jehovah Nissi as our conquering King.

I learned from Holy Spirit and the scriptures that everything that our savior won for us on Calvary's cross was already mine. I began to look for Him to guide me and protect me as my triumphant warrior during every situation that I would face as Senior Pastor at our church. Even when a situation looked impossible in the natural realm, I learned to expect miracles from Him.

One day, I began to feel very strongly in my spirit that our church was supposed to add a new sanctuary to our existing building. There were several prophets that came into our church and confirmed to me that the present walls were going to be moved and expanded out. Well, in the natural realm I knew that this would be impossible because there were wetlands on our property that could not be touched according to the laws in our town. In order to build we would need additional parking spaces that would impact the wetlands. But I did believe that God was saying in my spirit that we would be able to expand.

After some time passed, I received two post cards, one on my desk at church and one in my mailbox at home from the same company informing me that they had a sale on various sizes of steel frame buildings that we could use to build a new addition to our church. This was definitely a sign to me from God that we were supposed to build, so I began to pray and ask our intercessors to help seek clarity from God about something that seemed impossible in the natural realm.

Our town has a law on the books that says for us to build a larger sanctuary, we would need one parking space for every three people and I understood that we were now at our limit of parking spaces already. Therefore, we could not add a new sanctuary that would seat 600 to 800 more people. But this was not what I believe that God was saying to me. He said we were going to build!

One Sunday morning during our worship service, I heard the Spirit of God direct me to take the entire congregation outside to pray and to pour the Holy Communion meal into the wetlands and declare as the representative of Christ Jesus that in His name the wetlands would change to buildable land so that we could obey Him and build our new edifice. We all obeyed the Lord's executive orders that day.

Several months later I heard the Lord speak to me again and this time He instructed me to hire a soil scientist to come out and check the land so that we could take a new aerial map picture to town hall because there was already a map of our property filed there that showed the wetlands that were on our property.

One of our leaders informed me that he had a good friend who was a soil scientist and that he would try to reach him and invite him to come to our church to meet with our building committee concerning our wetlands. Praise God, our member eventually was able to reach him because he had been out of town on vacation for over a month and had just gotten back. He told our member that he would be honored to come and speak with us at our next building committee meeting. We then found out that this gentleman had served at one time as our town's soil scientist. Look at how Jehovah Nissi was working on our behalf!

We have in our possession today both aerial maps that are completely different! What a miracle, no more wetlands where we needed additional parking spaces in order to build our 100 x 100 square foot new sanctuary. We would now have more than enough parking spaces to satisfy the town. Our church successfully went through many challenges in order to obey God and build, but Jehovah Nissi, our banner and protector, our triumphant warrior raised up a standard of total victory for our church's new building project.

It took a few years of successful warfare as the congregation continued to faithfully hold up this apostolic leader's hands in prayer and faith confessions of God's promises to us. We prevailed by using God's authority and power until we were given the certificate of occupancy from the town for us to move into our beautiful new sanctuary, giving all glory and honor to our faithful God, Jehovah Nissi.

Jehovah Nissi's banner represents God's cause. In the Old Testament dispensation when God said to His people to hold up His rod, or pole or His standard, this represented Jehovah Nissi's call to battle and His sign of deliverance, victory and salvation for His people. We must believe that when Jehovah Nissi shows up we will always, always win!

Let's go to an Old Testament Scripture that reveals Jehovah Nissi in a situation that also looks impossible to Moses who was also God's apostolic leader.

Exodus 17:8-16 (AMP)

8 Then came Amalek [descendants of Esau] and fought with Israel at Rephidim.

9 And Moses said to Joshua, Choose us out men and go out, fight with Amalek. Tomorrow I will stand on the top of the hill with the rod of God in my hand.

10 So Joshua did as Moses said and fought with Amalek; and Moses, Aaron, and Hur went up to the hilltop.

11 When Moses held up his hand, Israel prevailed; and when he lowered his hand, Amalek prevailed.

12 But Moses' hands were heavy and grew weary. So [the other men] took a stone and put it under him and he sat on it. Then Aaron and Hur held up his hands, one on one side and one on the other side; so his hands were steady until the going down of the sun.

13 And Joshua mowed down and disabled Amalek and his people with the sword.

14 And the Lord said to Moses, Write this for a memorial in the book and rehearse it in the ears of Joshua, that I will utterly blot out the remembrance of Amalek from under the heavens.

15 And Moses built an altar and called the name of it, The Lord is my Banner;

16 And he said, Because [theirs] is a hand against the throne of the Lord, the Lord will have war with Amalek from generation to generation.

Let's begin to get revelation from Holy Spirit concerning these verses of scripture. In *verses 8-9*, Moses was God's Old Testament Apostolic leader, he would give instructions to Joshua and the people of God concerning revelation given to him from Jehovah Nissi. God had spoken to the senior leader concerning their warfare against their enemy Amalek. Moses instructed that in the morning he would stand on the top of the hill with God's rod, which represented God's authority and power. Moses held the authority and power of God in his hand, and because of it, Moses was able to perform the miraculous for God's people.

Verse 10-11: When Moses held up his hand God's people prevailed against their enemy. Remember the word banner means standard, the rod of God, the authority and power of God. It is important that we remember it is Jehovah Nissi who caused the miraculous to take place during our warfare. It is Jehovah Nissi that we called upon in the same way during our building project over and over again.

There were several times when this leader's hand grew heavy and weary. I learned in *verse 12-13* that every leader needs help from his or her members to hold them up in prayer and faith confessions, and to provide faithful service through their spiritual gifts and finances in order to support God's vision and mission for the house. I certainly needed all my members at many various times during our building project warfare. The enemy tried everything he could to stop us from building our new sanctuary, but he could not.

These scriptures revealed God's standard for His victory for us. Moses found rest as long as others in leadership held up the Senior leader's hands and as long as they did, God's people won the battle against the enemy.

Every leader needs everyone's cooperation in the church in order to prevail. In our church we understand the importance of every member being placed within a specific ministry within the church so that they can know their individual and collective assignment in order to help the senior leader to hold up my hands in victory during every assignment given to us from the Lord.

Now, let's look at the assignment given to Moses for his ground troops. They were also anointed to mow down and destroy the enemy with God's sword while their senior leaders were on the mountain fighting a fixed fight!

The sword in the New Testament is one of the believer's pieces of armor revealed in Ephesians 6. The sword which is the Word of God through the Holy Spirit, protects us from all kinds of evil. Jehovah Nissi provides God's adequate authority and power to every believer released through His Indwelling Spirit and His Word.

The Spirit and Life (zoë) in God's Word has the highest frequency of creative authority and power. When spoken by a New Covenant believer, this causes God's Word to never ever return unto Him void or without accomplishing everything that God purposed. Therefore, "God's Spoken Word" will always prosper in what God originally sent it forth to do when we speak it in faith.

Verse 14: Moses was ordered by the Lord to write down God's instructions and teach them, especially to

Joshua. God had chosen him to be Moses' successor and Joshua would need to know God's will for His people. This is the reason why every senior leader must teach God's people consistently concerning his vision for their house. God wanted Joshua, who would be the new leader to remind the people about this truth that as He was with Moses so would He be with them. He also promised that even the remembrance of Amalek would be utterly blotted out of their remembrance. I can tell you that this statement is also true for Full Gospel because we only remember the faithfulness of God when we worship in our new sanctuary.

Verse 15: Jehovah always desires His people to build Him an altar and to meet Him there for intimacy, worship and instructions. The altar is where God's Glory realm dwells! We are made whole in His presence and under His protection. God instructed us to build a very large altar area in our new sanctuary so that many of us could lay before him together to receive his presence and get under his protection.

Moses called this altar "Jehovah Nissi – The Lord is my Banner, the Lord is the rod and victory in my hands; The Lord is my standard and the miraculous in my life." As long as the leader's hands were holding up God's authority and power, His people won! Praise Jehovah, He remains the same, yesterday, today and forever more.

When the enemy tries to come after the people of God, we are instructed to lift up the rod of God which represents Jehovah Nissi, our conquering God, our protector, our God of war!

Verse 16: Our God would close this chapter by revealing a powerful truth that every believer in Christ today should not ever forget. It is vital that we remember that anybody who comes up against God's people are coming up against the very throne of God. Because we are seated with Christ in heavenly place, this promise also includes every new covenant believer today.

We must never forget that Jehovah Nissi promised to warfare with their enemy from generation to generation! This promise also belongs to us in our generation. God's Banner over our heads is also His Hesed Agape unconditional love.

Saints of God, as long as God's people hold up God's rod and staff which is the authority and power of God's Word, we win the battle in every fight, because the war has already been won at Calvary's cross. In God's Covenant we have been given a name that guarantees us the victory every time we speak it in faith because His Blood prevails forever, and His angelic host fortifies us during every attack.

THE SEVEN REDEMPTIVE NAMES OF CHRIST JESUS

Please go with me to a scripture that will confirm this very important statement and will also reveal to us Jehovah Nissi in Psalm 20 (AMP).

Psalm 20 (AMP)

1 May the Lord answer you in the day of trouble! May the name of the God of Jacob set you up on high [and defend you];

2 Send you help from the sanctuary and support, refresh, and strengthen you from Zion;

3 Remember all your offerings and accept your burnt sacrifice. Selah [pause, and think of that]!

4 May He grant you according to your heart's desire and fulfill all your plans.

5 We will [shout in] triumph at your salvation and victory, and in the name of our God we will set up our banners. May the Lord fulfill all your petitions.

6 Now I know that the Lord saves His anointed; He will answer him from His holy heaven with the saving strength of His right hand.

7 Some trust in and boast of chariots and some of horses, but we will trust in and boast of the name of the Lord our God.

> *8 They are bowed down and fallen, but we are risen and stand upright.*
>
> *9 O Lord, give victory; let the King answer us when we call.*

Let's now receive revelation from Holy Spirit in our New Covenant about Jehovah Nissi. This next scripture reveals so much to us about God's promises. I have learned how vital it is that we understand why His rod and His staff which is God's all-powerful Word must come out of a new covenant believer's mouth if we are going to win every battle.

> *Hebrews 4:12*
>
> *12 For the Word that God speaks is alive and full of power [making it active, operative, energizing, and effective]; it is sharper than any two-edged sword, penetrating to the dividing line of the [a]breath of life (soul) and [the immortal] spirit, and of joints and marrow [of the deepest parts of our nature], exposing and sifting and analyzing and judging the very thoughts and purposes of the heart.*

The Lord's Sword, which is the Word of God is alive with the zoë life of God and full of dunamis power. God's spirit life is in His word, it is His creative power given to us.

THE SEVEN REDEMPTIVE NAMES OF CHRIST JESUS

God's Word releases His miraculous and His creativity into all three parts of our being. When we declare God's Word it goes through our spirit, soul and body, healing us and making us completely whole.

The rod of God in the hands of Moses revealed God's standard against the Egyptian magicians. It was also used to bring water out of a rock, so that God's people would drink supernaturally. Jehovah Nissi is the rock that every believer stands on; Christ Jesus is our solid rock. When a believer stands on the Rock (Christ Jesus) with the Rod (the Word of God) coming out of our mouth we always win!

We must always remember the fight is fixed; Jesus has already won the war! Make sure you don't have a mixture in your word. Speak God's Word only and not the words of the enemy.

God's Word is eternal, it cannot fail. God's Word will never disappear or dissipate. Hold up the rod of Jehovah Nissi and win every battle!

Let's get another revelation from a New Testament scripture that reveals Jehovah Nissi who is our Banner, Victor, Protector and Warrior.

Colossians 2:13-15

13 And you who were dead in trespasses and in the uncircumcision of your flesh (your sensuality, your sinful carnal nature), [God] brought to life together with [Christ], having [freely] forgiven us all our transgressions,

14 Having cancelled and blotted out and wiped away the handwriting of the note (bond) with its legal decrees and demands which was in force and stood against us (hostile to us). This [note with its regulations, decrees, and demands] He set aside and cleared completely out of our way by nailing it to [His] cross.

15 [God] disarmed the principalities and powers that were ranged against us and made a bold display and public example of them, in triumphing over them in Him and in it [the cross].

Every new covenant believer was already considered dead because of our sinful nature and under the curse that began after the fall of man in the Garden of Eden. Then God made us alive when we were born again in Christ. God cancelled and blotted out our sins with the precious Blood of Jesus and wiped away the record that contained every charge against us that began in the Garden of Eden. The law had legal decrees and demands against anyone who broke them. Our heavenly Father put the entire law and its curse on Christ Jesus and nailed it to the Cross. Jesus became the substitutionary sacrifice for mankind on

Calvary's Cross. He became our Banner, Victor, Protector and Warrior.

Let's get confirmation in scripture.

Galatians 3:13:14

13 Christ purchased our freedom [redeeming us] from the curse (doom) of the Law [and its condemnation] by [Himself] becoming a curse for us, for it is written [in the Scriptures], Cursed is everyone who hangs on a tree (is crucified);

14 To the end that through [their receiving] Christ Jesus, the blessing [promised] to Abraham might come upon the Gentiles, so that we through faith might [all] receive [the realization of] the promise of the [Holy] Spirit.

This scripture confirms that Jehovah Nissi became every New Covenant believer's banner over us and triumphant victor, protector and warrior because he loved us so much that he died for us.

Jesus became every New Covenant believer's new standard before God. Every blessing promised to Father Abraham now belongs to every non-Jew who were once called Gentiles and through our faith in Christ Jesus we also were blessed with the indwelling Spirit of the living God.

Let's once again look at the scripture that proves our total victory.

> *Colossians 2:15*
>
> *15 [God] disarmed the principalities and powers that were ranged against us and made a bold display and public example of them, in triumphing over them in Him and in it [the cross].*

This scripture reveals that God, our heavenly Father, disarmed the evil rulers and authorities of Satan that were hostile against God's people and shamed every one of them through Christ Jesus, our Jehovah Nissi, who is our banner, victor and triumphant warrior.

Don't forget his promise in the Old Covenant that revealed he would deal with our enemies, generation after generation. On Calvary's cross Jesus was revealed as our blood-stained banner, our victor, our new standard and protector. All that the God head is dwells within us right now revealed in Colossians 2:10 (AMP).

> *Colossians 2:10 (AMP)*
>
> *10And you are in Him, made full and having come to fullness of life [in Christ you too are filled with the Godhead—Father, Son and Holy Spirit—and reach full spiritual stature]. And He is the Head of*

all rule and authority [of every angelic principality and power].

The Godhead lives in every New Covenant believer and Christ Jesus is the Head (Lord) over every ruler and authority in the universe. Jehovah Nissi is our banner and victor in warfare. I learned through the testing of my faith, as we walked through our new building project that nothing is impossible with God to them who believe him. We must remember that Jesus declared this on Calvary's Cross: "It is finished."

It is finished! Let us close with these words from I Corinthians 15:57-58 (AMP).

I Corinthians 15:57-58

57 But thanks be to God, Who gives us the victory [making us conquerors] through our Lord Jesus Christ.

58 Therefore, my beloved brethren, be firm (steadfast), immovable, always abounding in the work of the Lord [always being superior, excelling, doing more than enough in the service of the Lord], knowing and being continually aware that your labor in the Lord is not futile [it is never wasted or to no purpose].

Saints, because the Lord Jesus Christ is our banner and victor, there is no weapon even if it is formed against us, because of Christ Jesus, it cannot prosper! In Jesus Name, He showed Himself faithful to me and Full Gospel. Even though Satan had many plans to stop us from obeying God's prophetic word concerning building Him a larger sanctuary. He desired a place where many could come to hear the teachings of His gospel of grace and to receive revelation about His healing power available for the entire body of Christ. God did the miraculous, when we placed the powerful Holy Communion elements in the soil of our wetlands and spoke God's Spirit-filled words.

I believe that when we obeyed God the element became the literal body and blood of Christ Jesus. The resurrection power of God changed the soil in the wetlands and allowed Full Gospel to build our new sanctuary on buildable ground. We would now have enough parking spaces that would satisfy the rules of our town's ordinances because Jehovah Nissi, our redeemer, fought our battle. We won this triumphant victory all because His banner over us was love.

Saints, walk in this Covenant provision everyday victoriously healed, whole, and delivered from the entire assignment of the enemy. This assignment from the enemy includes sin and sickness, poverty and lack, and fear and failure. Jesus, our Jehovah

Nissi is watching over His Word to perform it in our daily lives. As we declare God's Covenant promises as our final authority because of Jehovah Nissi, we win every battle because the fight is fixed!

7 JEHOVAH TISIDKENU: GOD'S GIFT OF RIGHTEOUSNESS

JEHOVAH TISIDKENU IS the next Redemptive Name of Christ Jesus. Tisidkenu means Jehovah our "Righteous." Every New Covenant believer is righteous by faith through the finished works of Calvary's Cross. Righteousness is the gift of God. Jesus didn't come to cover our sins in order to make a believer righteous, but Christ Jesus came to "take away and completely blot out" the sins of the world. His Righteousness is our gift.

Romans 9:30-33

30 What shall we say then? That Gentiles who did not follow after righteousness [who did not seek salvation by right relationship to God] have attained it by faith [a righteousness imputed by God, based on and produced by faith],

31 Whereas Israel, though ever in pursuit of a law [for the securing] of righteousness (right standing with God), actually did not succeed in fulfilling the Law.

32 For what reason? Because [they pursued it] not through faith, relying [instead] on the merit of their works [they did not depend on faith but on what they could do]. They have stumbled over the Stumbling Stone.

33 As it is written, Behold I am laying in Zion a Stone that will make men stumble, a Rock that will make them fall; but he who believes in Him [who adheres to, trusts in, and relies on Him] shall not be put to shame nor be disappointed in his expectations.

Jehovah Tisidkenu reveals God's gift of righteousness by faith through every New Covenant believer. We cannot earn it, we do not deserve it, we cannot do anything to merit it; God's righteousness is a free gift of God to every New Covenant believer.

Once I received this biblical truth from Holy Spirit and the Word of God concerning how God's gift of righteousness was freely given to every male and female New Covenant believer, it changed my life forever.

In 1994, I made a life-changing decision to believe and obey God's prophetic call on my life to become the senior pastor of our Full Gospel Church. My husband and I obeyed God and pioneered our church by beginning our ministry in a community center.

I must admit that for several years I still fought the spirit of fear of rejection that I had during those early years of ministry. I tried to push my husband into the senior pastor's position because I really believed in those days that more men would join our ministry if there was a man in the senior position. You must understand in our area of the country there were no female senior pastors that I knew about. The women who had pastors for husbands were all called first ladies and not pastors. Well, my husband was not allowing it, he knew that God called him to stand beside me in ministry but not as the senior leader.

God also began to deal with me, and He began proving to me from scripture that He does not choose our call according to gender but that I was as much a righteous Son of God as my husband was. He revealed to me in scripture that before He formed me in my mother's womb, He chose me and planned for my purpose in ministry and finished me before He sent me to earth. I now understand from revelation given to me by Holy Spirit in this next scripture that God's gift of righteousness has positioned every believer in Christ to reign on earth as a royal priest and king regardless of our gender. Let's get revelation from Romans 5:17 (AMP).

> *Romans 5:17 (AMP)*
>
> *17 For if because of one man's trespass (lapse, offense) death reigned through that one, much more surely will those who receive [God's] overflowing grace (unmerited favor) and the free gift of righteousness [putting them into right standing with Himself] reign as kings in life through the one Man Jesus Christ (the Messiah, the Anointed One).*

This redemptive gift of God, through Christ Jesus is the master key that unlocks every Covenant blessing in the Kingdom of God here on earth. The Kingdom of God is within us as we reign as royal kings and priests on earth in Christ Jesus.

When you and I understand what God's gift of righteousness really means we will walk in our God given inheritance of righteousness daily, we will stop living below our covenant benefits. We should arise every new day declaring, "I am the righteousness of God in Christ Jesus," through Jehovah Tisidkenu our righteous king.

God's Word commands us to get His wisdom and His understanding as the most important things. Holy Spirit spent a lot of time with me in the Word of God during those early years of ministry revealing how the traditions of men often misinterpreted God's Word by taking it out of context. There are many denominational misbeliefs in the Church concerning women called to the five-fold ministry gifts given by God. I observed many women in those days bound by tradition and I was determined that it would no longer be me or any other woman that God would bring across my path that was afraid to become all that God called her to be according to Ephesians 1:4-6 (AMP).

Ephesians 1:4-6 (AMP)

4 Even as [in His love] He chose us [actually picked us out for Himself as His own] in Christ before the foundation of the world, that we should be holy (consecrated and set apart for Him) and blameless in His sight, even above reproach, before Him in love.

5 For He foreordained us (destined us, planned in love for us) to be adopted (revealed) as His own

> *children through Jesus Christ, in accordance with*
> *the purpose of His will [ª]because it pleased Him*
> *and was His kind intent]—*
>
> *6 [So that we might be] to the praise and the com-*
> *mendation of His glorious grace (favor and mercy),*
> *which He so freely bestowed on us in the Beloved.*

I have been told by many female ministers that my conse-
cration to the apostleship level set them free in this area.
Many now believe that they can be used by God in whatever capacity they believe God called them to. I studied
the scriptures led by Holy Spirit as He revealed to me all
the women of the bible that God called to the fivefold
offices in the Church. The Apostle Paul used many of
them in his own ministry. The spirit of God used me several
years ago to write my first book entitled, *That They May*
be One in Christ. The book revealed the names and ministry positions held by many females called by God and
used by the Holy Spirit to take the Gospel of the Kingdom to the world. It was the Apostle Paul who gave us
this next life-changing scripture that includes women
called by God.

> *Galatians 3:26-29*
>
> *26 For in Christ Jesus you are all sons of God*
> *through faith.*

27 For as many [of you] as were baptized into Christ [into a spiritual union and communion with Christ, the Anointed One, the Messiah] have put on (clothed yourselves with) Christ.

28 There is [now no distinction] neither Jew nor Greek, there is neither slave nor free, there is not male and female; for you are all one in Christ Jesus.

29 And if you belong to Christ [are in Him Who is Abraham's Seed], then you are Abraham's offspring and [spiritual] heirs according to promise.

In Christ Jesus there is no longer male and female according to spiritual things, but all are Sons of God through our faith in Christ Jesus.

This next scripture reveals God's biblical definition of the importance of getting his wisdom and understanding for our lives.

Proverbs 4:7

7 The beginning of Wisdom is: get Wisdom (skillful and godly Wisdom)! [For skillful and godly Wisdom is the principal thing.] And with all you have gotten, get understanding (discernment, comprehension, and interpretation).

Holy Spirit desires to give us revealed insights which is an understanding of "who we are right now in Christ Jesus!" God's gift makes us eternally righteous forever; this is our new identify in Christ.

The scriptures teach us that the first Adam brought death, but the last Adam, Christ Jesus, brought God's overflowing grace and the free gift of righteousness. According to God's Word we rule and reign on earth in Christ as both male and female royal Priests and Kings unto Christ Jesus.

Holy Spirit wants us to understand that before we were born again, we were not righteous but right now and for the rest of our entire lives here on earth we are eternally, the righteousness of God in Christ Jesus because of Jehovah Tisidkenu, our righteous king and high priest.

When a believer gets understanding about our free gift of righteousness, we will have faith in this truth and develop an understanding that we cannot lose it. We are not righteous because we were good, we are righteous because of our eternal position in Christ Jesus.

Let us receive more truth about our righteousness through this next scripture.

Ephesians 2:5-6

5 Even when we were dead (slain) by [our own] shortcomings and trespasses, He made us alive to-

*gether in fellowship and in union with Christ; [He
gave us the very life of Christ Himself, the same
new life with which He quickened Him, for] it is by
grace (His favor and mercy which you did not deserve) that you are saved (delivered from judgment
and made partakers of Christ's salvation).*

*6 And He raised us up together with Him and made
us sit down together [giving us joint seating with
Him] in the heavenly sphere [by virtue of our being]
in Christ Jesus (the Messiah, the Anointed One).*

We are seated with Christ in our new life in Him! His
righteousness qualifies us to become partakers of our full
inheritance in Christ.

Many years later, Holy Spirit began to reveal to me
the apostolic call on my life. I tried to ignore it for a long
time, but I could not deny that there was a definite
change in my level of revelation during my study time
with Holy Spirit and my teaching messages that He gave
me to share with the Body of Christ. My ability to hear
the voice of Holy Spirit increased tremendously and there
were several ministries that approached me to become
their spiritual apostolic covering.

Soon I would go to my chief apostle to share my
thoughts with him and to seek God's wisdom from him
concerning how to handle this next level in my call. He
informed me that God had given him a vision three

months prior to my visit that I should allow him to consecrate me to the governmental office of Apostle. He stated that God showed him that there would be many things I would do and places I would go that he had never been. You cannot imagine the fear I felt that day because I did not know of any female apostles in our region, but Holy Spirit reminded me about the female apostles that served with the Apostle Paul that I had studied and written about in my first book. I believe they were recorded in the Bible, but I never imagined that God would call me to be a present-day apostle for Christ Jesus.

Our Heavenly Father is so faithful because He began to connect me with so many male and female apostles that embraced the apostolic call on their lives. I am so grateful to my heavenly Father and the teaching ministry of Holy Spirit because of my obedience to search the scripture I am in my rightful place of ministry. God has led me to help so many find their place in ministry. To God be the glory for many of my new sons and daughters, who, to this very day refer to me affectionately as Mom Fortson and some of them have accepted me as their apostolic covering today.

God's gift of righteousness is the master key that unlocks the endless treasures of God's abundant grace. Grace and truth came by Christ Jesus, Jehovah Tisidkenu is our Righteous King and Savior.

THE SEVEN REDEMPTIVE NAMES OF CHRIST JESUS

It is vital that we believe Ephesians 2:7-9 (AMP).

Ephesians 2:7-9 (AMP)

7 He did this that He might clearly demonstrate through the ages to come the immeasurable (limitless, surpassing) riches of His free grace (His unmerited favor) in [His] kindness and goodness of heart toward us in Christ Jesus.

8 For it is by free grace (God's unmerited favor) that you are saved (delivered from judgment and made partakers of Christ's salvation) through [your] faith. And this [salvation] is not of yourselves [of your own doing, it came not through your own striving], but it is the gift of God;

9 Not because of works [not the fulfillment of the Law's demands], lest any man should boast. [It is not the result of what anyone can possibly do, so no one can pride himself in it or take glory to himself.]

God's supernatural force of righteousness will transform us as we continually come into the presence of God (Jehovah Shammah) daily. There is no end to the Lord's immeasurable, unlimited and surpassing power of His free grace within us. This grace Gift is our covenant blessing, purchased by the precious blood of Jesus. When we walk in the truth of Christ Jesus, we are setting ourselves free to receive and now we qualify to help set others free through God's abundant grace and truth because of John 1:16-17 (AMP).

> *John 1:16-17 (AMP)*
>
> *16 For out of His fullness (abundance) we have all received [all had a share and we were all supplied with] one grace after another and spiritual blessing upon spiritual blessing and even favor upon favor and gift [heaped] upon gift.*
>
> *17 For while the Law was given through Moses, grace (unearned, undeserved favor and spiritual blessing) and truth came through Jesus Christ.*

Let's get revelation from Holy Spirit about God's Promise to send Jehovah Tisidkenu to His people in this Old Testament scripture.

> *Jeremiah 23:5-6*
>
> *5 Behold, the days are coming, says the Lord, when I will raise up to David a righteous Branch (Sprout), and He will reign as King and do wisely and will execute justice and righteousness in the land.*

*6 In His days Judah shall be saved and Israel shall
dwell safely: and this is His name by which He shall
be called: The Lord Our Righteousness.*

This redemptive name prophesied in this Old Testament
scripture about the coming of our Lord Jesus Christ as
our righteous Savior was fulfilled in Matthew 1:21-25.

Matthew 1:21-25

*21 She will bear a Son, and you shall call His name
Jesus [the Greek form of the Hebrew Joshua, which
means Savior], for He will save His people from
their sins [that is, prevent them from failing and
missing the true end and scope of life, which is
God].*

*22 All this took place that it might be fulfilled which
the Lord had spoken through the prophet,*

*23 Behold, the virgin shall become pregnant and
give birth to a Son, and they shall call His name
Emmanuel—which, when translated, means, God
with us.*

*24 Then Joseph, being aroused from his sleep, did
as the angel of the Lord had commanded him: he
took [her to his side as] his wife.*

> 25 But he had no union with her as her husband
> until she had borne her firstborn Son; and he called
> His name Jesus.

The word righteousness means to be justified and in right standing with God, to be declared valid, to have a sound relationship between God and a believer, uprightness, to have a covenant between God and His people.

God's gift of righteousness is our legal deliverance from sinfulness and condemnation. God gives His righteousness as His gift to the person of faith. God reckons or credits a person justified or righteous on the basis of their faith in Christ Jesus.

God's righteousness is the power of God at work saving humanity through their faith in Christ Jesus. Righteousness is an unmerited, undeserved and unearned gift from God to all believers in Christ. Righteousness depends on the concrete activity of God towards us. God dealt with the sin of humanity through His Son Christ Jesus and at the same time healed all our diseases, so that we can be made whole. This gift of righteousness set us in the position to believe that we have a right to divine health and God's divine life.

God's justification is the entrance point for transformation which makes a believer right with God through the finished works of Calvary's Cross. The Lord's all powerful blood made our righteousness possible. This next scripture is solid proof of God's gift of righteousness given to every believer as we release our faith in Christ Jesus our righteous judge. Jehovah Tisidkenu fulfills God's complete purpose for our lives, He made us whole in Christ Jesus our Lord through the finished works of Calvary's Cross. It is time that every one of us believes every covenant promise from God in Romans 3:20-30 (AMP).

Romans 3:20-30 (AMP)

20 For no person will be justified (made righteous, acquitted, and judged acceptable) in His sight by observing the works prescribed by the Law. For [the real function of] the Law is to make men recognize and be conscious of sin [not mere perception, but an acquaintance with sin which works toward repentance, faith, and holy character].

21 But now the righteousness of God has been revealed independently and altogether apart from the Law, although actually it is attested by the Law and the Prophets,

22 Namely, the righteousness of God which comes by believing with personal trust and confident reliance on Jesus Christ (the Messiah). [And it is meant] for all who believe. For there is no distinction,

23 Since all have sinned and are falling short of the honor and glory which God bestows and receives.

24 [All] are justified and made upright and in right standing with God, freely and gratuitously by His grace (His unmerited favor and mercy), through the redemption which is [provided] in Christ Jesus,

25 Whom God put forward [before the eyes of all] as a mercy seat and propitiation by His blood [the cleansing and life-giving sacrifice of atonement and reconciliation, to be received] through faith. This was to show God's righteousness, because in His divine forbearance He had passed over and ignored former sins without punishment.

26 It was to demonstrate and prove at the present time (in the now season) that He Himself is righteous and that He justifies and accepts as righteous him who has [true] faith in Jesus.

27 Then what becomes of [our] pride and [our] boasting? It is excluded (banished, ruled out entirely). On what principle? [On the principle] of doing good deeds? No, but on the principle of faith.

28 For we hold that a man is justified and made upright by faith independent of and distinctly apart from good deeds (works of the Law). [The observance of the Law has nothing to do with justification.]

29 Or is God merely [the God] of Jews? Is He not the God of Gentiles also? Yes, of Gentiles also,

30 Since it is one and the same God Who will justify the circumcised by faith [which germinated from Abraham] and the uncircumcised through their [newly acquired] faith. [For it is the same trusting faith in both cases, a firmly relying faith in Jesus Christ].

Through Jehovah Tisidkenu, our free gift of righteousness empowers every believer to live an abundant life of grace and truth in Christ Jesus restoring us back to our Creator and covenant God. We have all rights and privileges with God, but we must remember, as indicated in *verse 28* that we are righteous by faith and not by the works of the law. Make sure you declare that "you are the righteousness of God in Christ Jesus," every day forgiven, healed, and made whole by our righteous king, Jehovah Tisidkenu.

8 JEHOVAH RAPHA: GOD'S DIVINE HEALER AND DELIVERER

J EHOVAH RAPHA IS the next redemptive name of Christ Jesus. Rapha means "Jehovah heals. It also means I AM the Lord that health thee, and I AM the Lord your great physician."

Jehovah Rapha is God's covenant promise for every New Covenant believer. The substitutionary sacrifice of Jesus on Calvary's cross was done to restore us and heal us spirit, soul and body. Scripture teaches us that this was done on Calvary's cross to make every believer whole in Christ

Jesus. Holy Spirit is going to give us some powerful revelations about Jehovah Rapha that will build our faith in
the finished works of Calvary's cross pertaining to divine
health and divine healing. After having my supernatural
encounter with God in January 1984, my spiritual walk
with Christ began to change. Not only was I preparing for
a full-time ministry, but it was very important that I
receive a new level of understanding about God's covenant promises for divine healing and health based on the
finished works of the cross.

That morning of January of 1984, my heavenly Father
promised me that He would teach me how to get my body
healed. He would begin to reveal to me how to get the
false beliefs out of my mind and how to get the truth of
God into my spirit man. I began to understand my legal
rights to walk in divine health and wholeness in Christ
because this was my birthright.

The more Holy Spirit taught me about my new and
better covenant, with better promises I began to understand why Satan was attacking my life so much especially
in the area of my health.

There was a call on my life that would expose his lies
to the Body of Christ because he was trying to convince
me that I could not get healed. How many know that the
devil is a liar!

THE SEVEN REDEMPTIVE NAMES OF CHRIST JESUS

I finally began to see in scripture that the precious body and blood of Jesus took care of all my needs on Calvary's cross. It was time for me to receive revelation knowledge from God's spirit, my supernatural teacher about the importance of inviting Jehovah Rapha into my life daily. I began to study about Christ the healer and found out that he is the one responsible and the one who qualifies for our divine healing and health. He took care of everything for the new covenant believer on Calvary's cross.

Saints, I had a lot of areas in my life that needed to be healed. I began to develop my faith in God's supernatural ability to make me whole for the first time in my life. Let us begin to receive some powerful revelation in a few Old Testament scriptures.

> *Psalm 107:19-20*
>
> *19 Then they cry to the Lord in their trouble, and He delivers them out of their distresses.*
>
> *20 He sends forth His word and heals them and rescues them from the pit and destruction.*

Our Lord Jesus Christ always hears us when we cry out to Him in faith. Jesus has a present-day ministry in every believer's life. He watches over His Word to perform it when we are going through our tests and trials. He promised to deliver us from all our distresses because He carried them all in His body on the cross at Calvary for us.

Our Heavenly Father's divine covenant plan is to heal His people from every sickness and disease, both physical and mental. The precious blood of Jesus paid it all. Our creator has always had a Covenant of healing for His people. Let's go to the next Old Testament scriptures.

Exodus 15:26

26 Saying, If you will diligently hearken to the voice of the Lord your God and will do what is right in His sight, and will listen to and obey His commandments and keep all His statutes, I will put none of the diseases upon you which I brought upon the Egyptians, for I am the Lord Who heals you.

He promised that He would not put on His people any of the diseases that He had put upon the Egyptians if they would keep His commandments.

Exodus 23:25 (AMP)

25 You shall serve the Lord your God; He shall bless your bread and water, and I will take sickness from your midst.

Deuteronomy 7:15 (AMP)

15 And the Lord will take away from you all sickness, and none of the evil diseases of Egypt which you knew will He put upon you but will lay them upon all who hate you.

God entered into a covenant with His people that included their deliverance and guaranteed their healing. Not one of His people left Egypt feeble or sick on the day of their Exodus out of Egypt.

Psalms 105:37 (AMP)

37 He brought [Israel] forth also with silver and gold, and there was not one feeble person among their tribes.

The word feeble means no one had any infirmities, no sicknesses or diseases, no physical weaknesses, illnesses or afflictions. We must also note that not one of the Israelites who left Egypt as a slave, left there sick or poor. The Spirit of Jehovah Rapha and Jehovah Jireh brought God's people forth out of slavery both healthy and wealthy! God promised His people that He would send His spoken word in the person of His living word Christ Jesus in the flesh.

While I was trying to obey God and build our church, I came under some tremendous attacks of the enemy. I began to experience a lot of stress and anxiety. I didn't realize that I had taken my eyes off Jesus who was my Jehovah Jireh. I got my eyes focused on the day-to-day responsibilities of a senior pastor. My emotions became very toxic and began to trigger a bad outbreak of eczema which also led to a sciatic nerve attack in my back and down both of my legs. One morning, I got up to use the bathroom and realized that I could not stand up straight. I was walking bent over facing the carpet and in so much pain that I began to cry out to God.

You cannot imagine how much fear came against my mind. Satan and every one of his assigned demons began to torment me with words like "you will be crippled all the rest of your life and now like the woman bowed over for 18 years, you will be also." I was able to make it into my bathroom, but because it has two levels, when I lifted my leg to step up, I lost my balance and fell back and hit the floor very hard. I was home alone that day so I had to crawl back to my bed and I laid there for hours and cried out to God in fear because all I could think about was how I was going to fulfill my ministry because of this demonic attack.

I was already going to a Christian chiropractor before this attack so when my husband finally came home, I asked him to call my doctor and make an appointment for me to see him right away. He told my husband to bring me right in that same day but because I could not walk without great pain, he had to get some of the men in our church to come and help me get into the car and then into the chiropractor's office. I did not know how the doctor would be able to get me onto the table to begin working on my back, but he assured me that with the help of God he was going to help me to come to full recovery.

I had to consistently remind myself through this very difficult process of recovery that the Lord promised that He would never leave me nor forsake me. Holy Spirit began to reveal to me that Jesus healed them all while he walked the earth in ministry and that this was my new covenant birthright. So, I began to study this next scripture so I could build my faith for total restoration in my body. Go with me to Matthew 4:23-24 (AMP).

Matthew 4:23-24 (AMP)

23 And He went about all Galilee, teaching in their synagogues and preaching the good news (Gospel) of the kingdom, and healing every disease and every weakness and infirmity among the people.

> *24 So the report of Him spread throughout all Syria, and they brought Him all who were sick, those afflicted with various diseases and torments, those under the power of demons, and epileptics, and paralyzed people, and He healed them.*

Let's now go to another very important Old Testament scripture that reveals Jehovah Rapha. This scripture set me free from my false belief about divine healing and health.

> *Isaiah 53:4-5 (AMP)*
>
> *4 Surely He has borne our griefs (sicknesses, weaknesses, and distresses) and carried our sorrows and pains [of punishment], yet we [ignorantly] considered Him stricken, smitten, and afflicted by God [as if with leprosy].*
>
> *5 But He was wounded for our transgressions, He was bruised for our guilt and iniquities; the chastisement [needful to obtain] peace and well-being for us was upon Him, and with the stripes [that wounded] Him we are healed and made whole.*

I want to give you some of the very important revelations that Holy Spirit taught me in this very powerful scripture.

Verse 4: Scripture prophecies that Christ Jesus through His substitutionary sacrifice on Calvary's cross has (past tense) borne our (not His) griefs (Hebrew: sicknesses, weaknesses and distresses) and carried our (not His) sorrows and pains (of punishment). Jesus was the only one who qualified to be punished for our sicknesses and sins. Jesus fulfilled this prophecy on Calvary's cross.

Saints, because Jesus was punished for us, we don't have to be punished with sicknesses, diseases, weaknesses, distresses, sorrows or pain. This would be called double jeopardy in the courts of Heaven. Holy Spirit taught me that we cannot be prosecuted for the same offense twice because Jesus died for us and as us on the Cross.

The Bible reveals to us that our heavenly Father made Jesus to be sin for us on the cross, but He never sinned in His flesh because His nature had no sin in His blood. He did not have natural blood in His body, His father was not of this world, so Jesus decided to become sin for us. God's life was in His sinless blood. When Christ Jesus went to the cross, He took all the curse that was caused by the First Adam when he sinned in the Garden and because we no longer qualified because of our sin nature, Jesus the last Adam died for us. Now it would be illegal for Satan to put any of the curses on us. Now through the blessings of Father Abraham we have been endowed with God's grace gift of eternal righteousness because of the Lord's substitutionary sacrifice on Calvary's cross.

Jesus is our Lamb of God who bore our sicknesses and all our sins. He became our scapegoat and carried all our sorrows and pains of punishments that we deserved. He was the only one who qualified and fulfilled the sacrificial Jewish Laws for us.

Verse 5: Jesus was (past tense) wounded for our (not His) transgressions (sins). He never sinned, He became sin for our (past, present and future) sins by his abundant gift of grace.

Jesus was (past tense) bruised (crushed) for our (not His) guilt and iniquities. The word iniquity is the root talking about our old sin nature which includes every generational curse and the sins of our forefathers. The chastisement (punishment) for us was upon Him, so that we could obtain God's peace and well-being (Shalom) which means wholeness, completeness, divine health and prosperity. The Lord's peace promises that there will be nothing missing, nothing broken and nothing lacking in our lives because of our Lord's finished works on Calvary's cross. This is our Lord's promise to every new covenant believer.

John 14:27

27 Peace I leave with you; My [own] peace I now give and bequeath to you. Not as the world gives do I give to you. Do not let your hearts be troubled,

*neither let them be afraid. [Stop allowing yourselves
to be agitated and disturbed; and do not permit
yourselves to be fearful and intimidated and cowardly and unsettled.]*

Do not ever forget that our Jehovah Rapha promised us
His shalom peace to every New Covenant believer. We
must also remember in Isaiah 53:5 that He prophesied
that with the stripes that wounded Jesus, (that crushed,
bruised and striped Him) you and I are healed and made
whole.

Holy Spirit will share revelation with us from this prophetic promise in Isaiah 53 and several New Testament
scriptures that will build our faith in the finished works of
Calvary's cross. It is time that we believe that Jehovah
Rapha has healed us and made us whole. Before the cross
Isaiah declared in Isaiah 53:5 that **we are** healed and
made whole. After the cross of Calvary scripture declares
in I Peter 2:24 that **we were** healed and made whole
which fulfilled the famous words of Jesus on the cross that
"It is Finished!"

Let's allow Holy Spirit to prove to us in scripture that
Isaiah 53 was fulfilled in Christ in a few New Testament
scriptures.

> Matthew 8:16-17
>
> 16 When evening came, they brought to Him many who were [a]under the power of demons, and He drove out the spirits with a word and restored to health all who were sick.
>
> 17 And thus He fulfilled what was spoken by the prophet Isaiah, He Himself took [[b]in order to carry away] our weaknesses and infirmities and bore [c]away our diseases.

Jehovah Rapha is revealed in this scripture. Note that this scripture declares that all were healed during Jesus' ministry.

Let's now see how Jehovah Rapha is revealed in this next scripture.

Verse 16: Jesus drove out demons with a word, Jesus was the Word spoken of in John 1:1 (AMP).

> John 1:1 (AMP)
>
> In the beginning [before all time] was the Word (Christ), and the Word was with God, and the Word was God Himself.

Jesus restored all who came to him with any kind of sickness and disease with his zoë life. Jesus could make no exceptions but to heal them all because it was our sicknesses and our diseases and our demonic oppressions that He bore for us on the cross. Jesus did this in order to fulfill Isaiah's prophecy, He healed them all.

Matthew declares that this verse fulfilled Isaiah 53:4. Jesus took upon Himself all our weaknesses and all our infirmities, and all our diseases.

In the substitutionary chapter in Isaiah 53, our Redeemer bore our weakness and infirmities. This includes our sicknesses, diseases, illnesses, physical weaknesses, feebleness, failing health, afflictions and frailties. Jesus bore and carried away as our Lamb and scapegoat all that the curse would provide. Jehovah Rapha always restores to divine health all who are sick and come to him by faith

It is vitally important for us to remember that our Heavenly Father is a legalist in the realm of the Spirit. These curses cannot be on Jesus and on a believer in Christ at the same time. What Jesus took on His cross for us cannot legally be on us. We must rebuke every lie of Satan who is the author of all of the curse. Remember Jesus was our sacrifice. We must rebuke the enemy, this means to censor, forbid, and to not allow something illegal to take place in our lives.

Romans 8:11

> 11 And if the Spirit of Him Who raised up Jesus
> from the dead dwells in you, [then] He Who raised
> up Christ Jesus from the dead will also restore to
> life your mortal (short-lived, perishable) bodies
> through His Spirit Who dwells in you.

This is one of my favorite redemptive scriptures that reveals the finished works of Calvary's cross and Jehovah Rapha constantly at work in a believer's life.

The most important question to answer in this scripture is "Does the Spirit of God dwell in you?" If the answer is yes, then all the covenant promises in this verse belong to you now!

Every day we must expect His quickening power in our mortal bodies to keep us healed and make us whole. God's spirit dwells in us continuously and all we have to do is believe it and declare it.

Jehovah Rapha will restore you from the inside out when you put God's Word seed, by faith, in your heart.

> Mark 4:26-29
>
> 26 And He said, The kingdom of God is like a man
> who scatters seed upon the ground,
>
> 27 And then continues sleeping and rising night
> and day while the seed sprouts and grows and in-
> creases—he knows not how.

28 The earth produces [acting] by itself—first the blade, then the ear, then the full grain in the ear.

29 But when the grain is ripe and permits, immediately he sends forth [the reapers] and puts in the sickle, because the harvest stands ready.

The word "restore" in Romans 8 means to make our bodies whole with God's zoë life, and to bring it back to a former condition before the attack by Satan in order to repair it. It also means to establish divine order and to bring to divine health supernaturally. Holy Spirit dwells in our bodies every single minute of the day to quicken and permeate His divine zoë life in our veins. Keep God's Word in your reborn spirit and in your mouth for manifestation of God's promises.

The same Spirit that raised Jesus from the dead dwells in every believer and He desires to restore our mortal (physical) bodies to divine health so that we can bring glory to Him in our bodies. Let's prove it in scripture.

I Corinthians 6:19-20

19 Do you not know that your body is the temple (the very sanctuary) of the Holy Spirit Who lives within you, Whom you have received [as a Gift] from God? You are not your own,

> *20 You were bought with a price [purchased with a preciousness and paid for, made His own]. So then, honor God and bring glory to Him in your body.*

Our bodies are God's temples (sanctuaries) where Holy Spirit and faith substance dwells in our reborn spirits. The precious, sinless blood of Jesus purchased us, and we are commanded by God to bring honor and glory to our Creator in our bodies!

All of this is possible because of the indwelling work of Holy Spirit in us if we allow Him to quicken us daily with his zoë life. Scripture reveals to us that we receive this life when we eat His flesh and drink His blood every day during our Holy Communion meal. Please study this in John 6.

We can be made whole by allowing Jehovah Rapha freedom every day to have total charge over our bodies which scripture says is God's holy temples on earth.

This next scripture reveals that the prophetic promises we read about earlier in Isaiah 53:4-5 has been fulfilled.

> *I Peter 2:24*
>
> *24 He personally bore our sins in His [own] body on the tree [as on an altar and offered Himself on it], that we might die (cease to exist) to sin and live to righteousness. By His wounds you have been healed.*

Isaiah prophesized that we are healed (future tense) but now we see that (past tense) the Apostle Peter declares that we have been healed. This scripture in I Peter reveals that our complete redemption from the entire curse of the law has been fulfilled in Christ Jesus. We will walk in this entire promise when we do the same thing by putting the curse in past tenses. The Lord's sacrifice is complete and finished because of His precious blood.

Jesus died so that sin and sickness would no longer have dominion over a born-again believer because we are no longer under the curse of the law.

> *Romans 6:14*
>
> *14 For sin shall not [any longer] exert dominion over you, since now you are not under Law [as slaves], but under grace [as subjects of God's favor and mercy].*

We are now commanded to live in our new life and position in Christ through righteousness because the Holy Spirit has come to dwell in us.

> *John 16:7-11*
>
> *7 However, I am telling you nothing but the truth when I say it is profitable (good, expedient, advantageous) for you that I go away. Because if I do not*

> *go away, the Comforter (Counselor, Helper, Advo-*
> *cate, Intercessor, Strengthener, Standby) will not*
> *come to you [into close fellowship with you]; but if I*
> *go away, I will send Him to you [to be in close fel-*
> *lowship with you].*
>
> *8 And when He comes, He will convict and con-*
> *vince the world and bring demonstration to it about*
> *sin and about righteousness (uprightness of heart*
> *and right standing with God) and about judgment:*
>
> *9 About sin, because they do not believe in Me*
> *[trust in, rely on, and adhere to Me];*
>
> *10 About righteousness (uprightness of heart and*
> *right standing with God), because I go to My Fa-*
> *ther, and you will see Me no longer;*
>
> *11 About judgment, because the ruler (evil genius,*
> *prince) of this world [Satan] is judged and con-*
> *demned and sentence already is passed upon him.*

Jehovah Rapha promised these three things to every new covenant believer from the indwelling Holy Spirit:

Verse 9: Holy Spirit has revealed to me that one of His assignments on earth is to convict and convince the world that the only sin that a person will be judged for is the sin of unbelief, not trusting, relying or adhering to and believing in Christ Jesus as our Savior and Lord, and following God's ways according to what is right.

THE SEVEN REDEMPTIVE NAMES OF CHRIST JESUS

Before the foundation of the world Jesus decided to become the Lamb of God and be wounded for the world's transgressions, guilt and iniquities. All sin and our sin natures were put on Christ Jesus and anyone who would accept His substitutionary sacrifice on Calvary's cross would be forgiven and set free. So, it was our Lord's sin-less blood that paid the price in full to redeem us back to our creator. Therefore, the only sin that our heavenly Father can ever hold against us legally is the sin of not believing in Christ Jesus.

I personally learned from this scripture that a person does not go to hell for their sins but only for the one sin which is the sin of unbelief in the finished works of the cross. Jesus took care of every person's sin and our fallen nature on Calvary's cross and we are saved when we believe that the blood of Jesus paid it all. Let's look at this proof in Hebrews 9:12 (AMP).

Hebrews 9:12 (AMP)

12 He went once for all into the [Holy of] Holies [of heaven], not by virtue of the blood of goats and calves [by which to make reconciliation between God and man], but His own blood, having found and secured a complete redemption (an everlasting release for us).

His blood secured a complete redemption for us. Jehovah Rapha, our healer and deliverer, released us from the entire curse and all we have to do is believe in him and receive him by faith. This scripture in John 16:9 taught me the importance of building my faith in Christ and allowing Holy Spirit to uncover any unbelief in my heart.

The second assignment of Holy Spirit revealed in John 16:10 talks about the believer's righteousness.

Verse 10: Once Jesus returned to the Father after fulfilling His complete redemptive requirements every born-again believer has received the grace gift of righteousness. We have all rights and privileges in God's Kingdom.

This is every believer's new identity in Christ. When I found out who we are in Christ *right now*, I began to declare every day, "I am the righteousness of God in Christ Jesus." I began to believe, through the help of Holy Spirit, that I have right standing with my Creator every day; and that I really do hold dual citizenship on earth and in heaven because of God's eternal life in me. I began seeing myself seated beside Christ Jesus in the throne room of heaven. I began allowing Jesus to build my faith and my new identity of the righteousness of God in Christ Jesus. Thanks to the work of the Holy Spirit in me I noticed that my fears and phobias were quickly disappearing!

The third assignment of Holy Spirit revealed in *verse 11* is to teach us that we can shout the victory because

Satan is already judged, condemned and sentenced to complete destruction because of the finished works of Calvary's cross.

Holy Spirit helped me to get delivered from the spirit of fear by convincing me from scripture that the enemy to my faith was judged and condemned and sentenced to the lake of fire and brimstone. I now understand that I do not have to be afraid anymore because the author of the entire curse has no more power or authority over me unless I allow him to. I began to believe that no weapon—even if Satan formed it—can prosper against me. The blood of Jesus protects me and you, and Satan can no longer set up strongholds in our minds.

We must declare our righteous position in Christ every day. Holy Spirit gave me this powerful revelation from this next New Testament scripture in Revelation 20:10 (AMP).

Revelation 20:10 (AMP)

10 Then the devil who had led them astray [deceiving and seducing them] was hurled into the fiery lake of burning brimstone, where the beast and false prophet were; and they will be tormented day and night forever and ever (through the ages of the ages).

When Christ Jesus paid the price in full for our sins, His substitutionary sacrifice took care of everything that came against us through the curse that began in the Garden. Sin is what caused the curse, when Christ Jesus took care of sin with His sacrificial blood, He got rid of Satan's ability to put sin, sickness and death on a believer. This is why it is vital that we understand what Jesus has already done for us, He said It Is Finished and Jesus cannot lie! Scripture declares that "as Christ Jesus is right now in Heaven so are we right now on earth." We are the righteousness of God in Christ Jesus and are under a new spiritual law.

Let's go to Romans 8:1-2 (AMP).

Romans 8:1-2 (AMP)

1 Therefore, [there is] now no condemnation (no adjudging guilty of wrong) for those who are in Christ Jesus, who live [and] walk not after the dictates of the flesh, but after the dictates of the Spirit.

2 For the law of the Spirit of life [which is] in Christ Jesus [the law of our new being] has freed me from the law of sin and of death.

Every believer has died in Christ to sins, guilt, condemnation and eternal punishment. We have been gifted with a new, free life in Christ. There is a new law operating in us called "The Law of the Spirit of Zoë life in Christ." Jesus said the words I speak are spirit and zoë life. We have been (past tense) freed by the precious all-powerful blood of Christ Jesus from the curse of the law that brings sin, sickness and death. Remember the Bible says, "the wages that sin pays is still death which is eternal separation (the second death) from God our Creator."

These three assignments of Holy Spirit revealed in John 16:9-11 is the proof of our complete redemption in Christ Jesus. Our righteous position in Christ Jesus builds our faith because it is important that we do not operate in unbelief.

Holy Spirit has done an awesome job of teaching me about three types of power that dwells in every spirit filled believer's life. Jesus promised us this power in Acts 1:8.

The very first power given to a New Covenant believer is the all authority that was given to Jesus when He rose from the dead. Jesus declared, "all power and authority was given to me in heaven and on earth. Then Jesus turned around and gave His authority to His church to finish what he began on earth." The first type of power given to a believer is called *exousia* power. This is a believer's legal right as a royal king and priest in Christ to plead the blood of Jesus and declare the name of Jesus in warfare. We are anointed and appointed with this authority to rule, reign and dominate as an ambassador of Christ Jesus on earth. This authority empowers us to operate in the ministry of reconciliation. We have been commissioned to win sinners to Christ and to bring the Body of Christ to maturity.

The second type of power that Holy Spirit taught me about is called *kratos* power which is the supernatural ability of God to do the work of the ministry on earth. Holy Spirit empowers every believer through the supernatural ability of God to release signs and wonders and miracles. We are also commissioned through this *kratos* power to cast out devils, heal the sick and raise the dead.

The third type of power given by Christ to His Church is called *dunamis* power which is the might and supernatural strength of God in every believer. This *dunamis* power causes us to be able to supernaturally stand against every attack of the enemy successfully.

Jesus revealed an example of all three types of His God-given power at work in a New Covenant believer in Luke 10:19 (AMP).

Luke 10:19

19 Behold! I have given you authority and power to trample upon serpents and scorpions, and [physical and mental strength and ability] over all the power that the enemy [possesses]; and nothing shall in any way harm you.

Holy Spirit taught me through this scripture that the only type of power that Satan has against us is the ability to deceive us through his lies. Satan's authority (*exousia* has been stripped from him through the finished works of Calvary's cross.

Now every spirit-filled believer has a legal right through Christ Jesus to declare mastery over every attack of Satan. This is our birthright in Christ Jesus! We can legally walk in divine health and wholeness in spirit, soul, and body every day because of Jehovah Rapha.

We have every legal right to succeed in this life because of what Christ Jesus has already done for us through His seven redemptive names:

1. Jehovah Shammah – The Lord is our Ever-Present God
2. Jehovah Shalom – The Lord is our Peace and Well-being
3. Jehovah Rohi – The Lord is our chief Shepherd and Protector
4. Jehovah Jireh – The Lord is our Provider and Source

5. Jehovah Nissi – The Lord is our Banner, Victor and Triumphant Warrior

6. Jehovah Tisidkenu – The Lord is our Eternal Righteous Redeemer

7. Jehovah Rapha – The Lord is our Healer and Divine Health.

To every New Covenant believer, we can walk every day in our full inheritance in Christ Jesus, healthy and whole. Saints, our complete redemption through Christ Jesus is the currency of Heaven. The precious Blood of Jesus gives us access to every one of our New Covenant Provisions. Let us submit ourselves to the executive orders of our Commander and Chief and walk in every one of the seven covenant benefits of Christ Jesus every day!

Begin confessing the faith declarations in the next chapter daily. Fill your atmosphere with the truth found in God's eternal word. Speak them out of your mouth and walk in God's divine health, whole spirit, soul and body.

APPENDIX

OUR FAITH DECLARATIONS

BECAUSE OF THE seven redemptive names of Christ Jesus every New Testament Believer has inherited God's Covenant Benefits and provisions included in our Lord's Redemptive Names. We have been given the Executive Orders from Our Commander-in-Chief to transfer God's Covenant blessings from the supernatural realm into our lives daily by declaring God's Word. We are a speaking spirit recreated by God for the purpose of operating on earth in His image and likeness, to dominate and bring God's Kingdom to earth.

God expects His Executive Orders to be carried out by every New Covenant believer through the ministry of the Holy Spirit as we submit to Him every day making these faith declarations in our atmosphere:

Father in the Name of Christ Jesus, Jehovah Shammah is the Shekinah Glory and Supernatural Presence dwelling within me every day. I declare that no matter what is going on in my life today, I have legal access into the glory-realm of your manifested presence. I declare that I am seated with You, far above all of Satan's demonic powers. I have dual citizenship and have been assigned by you to cut off the powerlines, the communication lines and the supply lines of the devil again today. I declare that Jesus did destroy the works of the devil, therefore because of God's manifest Presence in my life, I have the victory every day in Jesus Name.

Father in the Name of Christ Jesus, I declare that Jehovah Shalom is the Perfect Peace and Well-being within me. I declare that Your Shalom Peace and Well-being has been given to me in abundance. Lord because of You my heart shall not be troubled or afraid. I declare that Your divine health, Your wholeness and completeness dwells within me bringing Your zoë life into my spirit, soul and body. I declare in Jesus Name that because of Your Peace and Well-being there is nothing missing, nothing lacking or broken in my life. I declare that I have complete confidence in You even in the midst of my test and trials because You have already conquered the enemy for me. I decree that I will rest in Your Shalom Peace and Well-being; your healing and health and I will be of good cheer again today because Your precious Blood has purchased my perfect peace and well-being in Jesus Name.

Father in the Name of Christ Jesus, I declare that Jehovah Rohi is my Chief Shepherd and Protector who gave His life for me. I decree that because the Lord is also my Caregiver when the thief comes against me, I will remember that my Chief Shepherd has already judged and sentenced the enemy for me. He has raised up a perfect standard against him. Lord you are trustworthy, and I am so grateful that You guide my footsteps and You protect my life from all danger, seen and unseen. As my Chief Shepherd You are the Source of my life and have given me the legal right to enjoy my life in abundance until it overflows in Jesus Name.

Father in the Name of Christ Jesus, I declare that Jehovah Jireh is my eternal Provider who meets my every need spirit, soul and body. Lord, I decree that You know what I have need of even before I know I need it. I declare that you meet my every need according to your riches in glory by Christ Jesus. I declare that Your will is being done here on earth in my life as it is being done right now in heaven. I declare that my eternal Provider causes all of

God's Covenant Blessings of Grace to come to me in abundance. In Jesus Name it is You Lord who provides seed for my sowing and bread for my eating. You multiply my resources so that I can increase supernaturally in every area of my life. I expect your supernatural provisions of forgiveness, healing and health, prosperity and wealth and total deliverance from the enemy every day in Jesus' Name.

Father in the Name of Christ Jesus, I declare that Jehovah Nissi is my Banner and Victorious Warrior. I declare that it is You Lord that always leads me in triumphant and victory over every situation and circumstance I will face in this life. I decree in Jesus Name that every time I hold up Your Banner, which is Your Word, the Rod of God, I always get the Victory. The fight is fixed, I win! I declare that there is no weapon, even if it's already formed, it cannot prosper against me. I have overcome Satan by the Blood of the Lamb and the declarations of Your Word. Your Word will not return unto You void; it will always prosper in my life. I decree Your Banner over me is always hesed agape love and triumphant victory in Jesus' Name!

THE SEVEN REDEMPTIVE NAMES OF CHRIST JESUS

Father in the Name of Christ Jesus I declare that Jehovah Tisidkenu is Your gift of Righteousness to me because of my faith in Christ Jesus, my Lord. I decree every day that I am the Righteousness of God in Christ Jesus. I have been justified, acquitted and declared righteous through my faith in the Finished Work of the Cross at Calvary. I declare that I have the Peace of Reconciliation to hold on to and enjoy every day. I declare that I have been brought back into a right relationship with You Abba Father by the precious blood of Your Son, Christ Jesus. I decree that I am delivered daily from the dominion of sin and sickness through Your gift of the resurrection power of Christ Jesus flowing in me. Because of Your Righteousness in me I have a Blood-bought right to access my full inheritance in Christ. I decree that I am reigning in this life as one of Your royal Priests adorned with Your Kingly anointing through Christ Jesus. I plead the Blood of Jesus as Your royal priests, and I declare Your eternal Word adorned as one of Your kings, in Jesus' Name.

Father in the Name of Christ Jesus I declare that Jehovah Rapha is my divine Physician, Healer and Deliverer. I declare that it was You Lord Jesus who bore in Your body for me every one of my sicknesses, weaknesses and distresses. You also carried all my sorrows and pains of punishments. Lord it was You who was wounded for all my sins: past, present and even future. It was You, Lord that was crushed for our guilt and iniquities, and for all the blood-line sins in our old nature. The punishment that needed to be paid for our peace and well-being was upon You. Therefore, Jesus, I know that in the courts of heaven I cannot be punished twice for the same crime, this would be called double jeopardy. Therefore, I declare again today Peace-Peace, nothing missing, broken or lacking. I declare total wholeness in every area of my life. Lord Jesus, because of the Blood in Your stripes I was healed two thousand years ago and made whole! Jesus, my blood cells are now carrying Your creative spirit-life throughout my body as I submit again today to the quickening Power of Your Spirit in me. You are my divine healer and deliverer in Jesus Name.

Today and every day of our lives here on earth you and I must obey our Commander-in-Chief's executive orders to declare all of God's New Covenant Blessings found in these Seven Redemptive Names of Christ Jesus, our Lord.

ABOUT THE AUTHOR

Apostle Cheryl A. Fortson is the founding Senior Pastor of Full Gospel Foundation Building Ministries International of Bloomfield, Connecticut.

Apostle Cheryl, affectionately referred to as "Mom Fortson" has been married to her Co-Pastor, John Fortson, Sr. since January 23, 1965. They are the proud parents of two sons and a daughter. John Jr. serves as the Children's Pastor and Darryl, Sr. serves as the Youth Pastor along with his wife, Prophet Christine. Their daughter, Chervon, serves as a deacon in the Church. They are also the proud grandparents of twelve anointed grandchildren and seven great grandchildren and several godchildren and spiritual sons and daughters all over the world. Apostle Cheryl is the Apostolic overseer of several churches.

Apostle Cheryl is known by many as a master teacher to the Body of Christ because she knows how to use the all-powerful Word of God to break up foul ground in the heart of the hearer. Apostle allows Holy Spirit to build a foundation in those whom she teaches. You can always hear Apostle Cheryl say, "Let us submit to the miraculous teaching ministry of Holy Spirit's revelation," before she teaches anything.

She is the founder and chancellor of the Perfecting School of Ministry which is the ministry's accredited bible training center, as well as Kingdom Business Academy and Bookstore where many believers are being perfected for their ministries. Also an entrepreneur, Apostle Cheryl owns several business within the church and is the CEO of *Cheryl A. Fortson Ministries LLC.*

She is the author of *That They May Be One in Christ* a profound teaching that focuses on bringing both the male and female Adam in Christ into Oneness. She also has many audio series available.

Apostle Cheryl is a national and international speaker and has helped her Chief Apostle plant an annual conference in Trinidad-Tobago every April and she is also the co-host of the New England Prophetic Conference held in Bloomfield, Connecticut every August.

THE SEVEN REDEMPTIVE NAMES OF CHRIST JESUS

Her life's desire is to reveal the heart of our Abba Father and the hesed agape love of Christ Jesus our Savior and Lord and the all-powerful daily ministry of Holy Spirit to this world through her ministry.

You can reach Apostle for ministry and resource materials at both the off-line and on-line addresses below:

42 East Dudley Town Road, Bloomfield, CT 06002
Administrative Department (860) 769-0505 Ext. 3

- Facebook: Full Gospel Foundation Building Ministries Intel.
- YouTube Channel: FGFBMI
- Ministry page: Cheryl A. Fortson Ministries, LLC
- Email address: apostlecheryl@comcast.net